The

COLLECTED

POEMS

of

C. P. CAVAFY

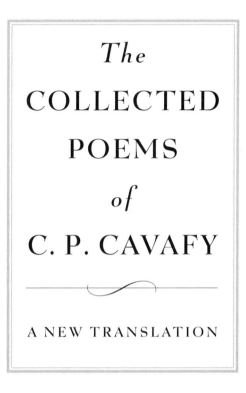

The
COLLECTED
POEMS
of
C. P. CAVAFY

A NEW TRANSLATION

Translated by Aliki Barnstone

W. W. NORTON & COMPANY

New York London

Copyright © 2006 by Aliki Barnstone
Foreword copyright © 2006 by W. W. Norton & Company, Inc.

Manufacturing by The Maple-Vail Book Manufacturing Group
Book design by JAM Design
Production manager: Anna Oler

Library of Congress Cataloging-in-Publication Data

Cavafy, Constantine, 1863–1933.
[Poems. English]
The collected poems of C. P. Cavafy : a new translation / translated by Aliki Barnstone.
p. cm.
Includes bibliographical references and index.
ISBN-13: 978-0-393-06142-0 (hardcover)
ISBN-10: 0-393-06142-6 (hardcover)
I. Barnstone, Aliki. II. Title.
PA5610.K2 A2 2006
889'.132—dc22   2005033685

W. W. Norton & Company, Inc., 500 Fifth Avenue, New York, N.Y. 10110
www.wwnorton.com

W. W. Norton & Company Ltd., Castle House, 75/76 Wells Street, London W1T 3QT

1 2 3 4 5 6 7 8 9 0

For my mother, Elli Tzalopoulou-Barnstone,

like Cavafy an exile from Constantinople,

and for my father, Willis Barnstone,

the first to share with me his love of Cavafy

CONTENTS

• 1932
Days of 1908 | *203*

• 1935
In the Suburbs of Antioch | *205*

FOREWORD

It was Auden who said, famously, in his introduction to Rae Dalven's Cavafy, that there were poems he would have written differently, or not at all, if he had not read Cavafy first, and I know this is true of myself and of others I could think of as well, yet I would hesitate to identify just what the influence was, whether an attitude to history, or a certain irony, or a use of *personae*, or a kind of passionate objectivity, or something else. What is interesting is that the poets I might refer to do not necessarily write like each other or even relate to one another. This I believe reflects the power of a major poet, his or her influence is shared by dissimilars, be it Stevens or Yeats or Rilke we are talking about. I think, if anything, it is a tender humanism, a *humanitas* supreme, we can identify particularly as Cavafy's.

It is this humanitas that emerges, *above* anything else, in the translations, and I would venture to say that one can measure the very degree of success of the translation by the keenness of retaining the original human feeling, that there is where the verisimilitude lies, or should lie. I am speaking of Cavafy's sensibility. Auden, for want of a better term—and he bespeaks his own inadequacy here—calls it a tone of voice and a personal speech. As Auden says, every *translation* of Cavafy, no matter by whom, "is immediately recognizable as a poem by Cavafy; nobody else could possibly have written it." It is, of all things, the "self-disclosure," the confession, that is translatable. The poem may have—and generally was—rhymed in the original, it contained a peculiar, unique, and totally original combination of "purist" and demotic Greek, but those things do not in any way emerge in the translations. In fact, we might assume a great, even a deadly, loss by their absence, by the fact that they were not translated, were the translations—by all hands—not so moving and so apparently accurate as they are. I must confess that I sometimes worry that we can't get the true Cavafy without what I'll call his *poetics* and his linguistics, but I thank God that all the major translators were wise enough not to make those things the object of their translations. How could they anyway?

I have compared the different translations to the best of my ability. One notices the difference—often very slight—and longs for the original. I have, of course, in poem after poem, moved from the literal to the poetic rendering and agonized over the difficulties as well as the difference between the "versions." The virtue of having a number of translations is obviously that one rendering, or interpretation, or structure, will be more accurate, or more delightful, than another—and the more minds at work the better. In different ways, I like the three major translations I own, Dalven, Keeley, and Theoharis, as well as their notes and their commentary, but I admire Aliki Barnstone's the most because it is, finally, a little less stiff and more lovely—and cunning—nearer what it seems to me the original might be and I love the extensive notes and the exhaustive commentary. Barnstone is a poet, and she is able to construct, to create—or re-create—the poem. There is, in addition, the magical connection (between poet and translator) that there always is. I'll call it a *sympathy,* a fellow-feeling, she shares, or she has, with Cavafy. She herself writes in English, but her father, the scholar, translator, and poet Willis Barnstone, is Jewish and her mother, the painter Elli Tzalopoulou-Barnstone, is Greek, so she has lived in a double-diaspora, in Nevada now, of all places, which gives her even more kinship with Cavafy.

This being said, I must add that in every translation, what comes through is a kind of aloofness, even a coldness, a distance let's call it, whether the subject be Hellenic-historical on the one hand or lyric-personal on the other. But I want to suggest that coldness is *not* the word, that the poems are *burning,* and that it is only his irony, his *ten-*

der irony, that saves them, as it were, from being consumed. Indeed they are heartbreaking poems. Carefully wrought, labored over, but heartbreaking. Sometimes he forgets the irony, the flimsy curtain or the light cover he seems to place on everything and he speaks "directly from the heart" as if he were some romantic fool or lost nostalgic. Look at this early poem:

VOICES

Ideal and loved voices
of the dead, or of those
lost to us like the dead.

Sometimes they speak to us in dreams;
sometimes the brain hears them in thought.

And, for one moment, with their sounds,
sounds come back from the first poetry of our lives—
like music at night, remote, fading away.

[1904]

or this later one, lest we assume rawness and vulnerability were issues of maturity:

IN DESPAIR

He's utterly lost him.   And now he seeks
his lips   in the lips
of each new lover;   in the union with each
new lover,   he seeks to fool himself
that he is the same young man,   the same one he gives himself to.

He's utterly lost him,   as if he never existed.
Because he wanted—he said—   he wanted to save himself
from the stigma   of that morbid pleasure,
from the stigma   of that shameful pleasure.
There was still time—   he said—to save himself.

He's utterly lost him,   as if he never existed.
In his fantasy,   in his hallucination,
he seeks his lips   in the lips of other young men;
he wants to feel   his passion again.

[1923]

Cavafy is not Rimbaud. He doesn't achieve his intensity, his purity of thought, through metaphor. In fact he eschews metaphor altogether, unless we see the whole poems as a kind of metaphoric wonder where one state magically becomes another. His style is loose and idiomatic, based on and explicating the educated speech of his native Alexandria. It is "learned" but only learned in the manner of a well-read, well-rounded citizen of that city, including that citizen's complacency and presumptuousness, though there is a sly crafty wild and sometimes brutal eye—and tongue—behind that citizen.

Like most of the other great moderns, Cavafy combines a certain conservatism with a poetic radicalism. But it is a conservatism based on hard-earned knowledge rather than loony economic and political ideas. He more or less rejects progressivism but there isn't one whiff of fascism or proto-fascism anywhere, unlike in, say, Yeats, Eliot, and Pound. In a poem published in 1928, certainly years after Mussolini's arrival and the mean scapegoating of the London, and Idaho, senescents, he argues against the Political Reformer (capitalized in the poem) in a gentle and sane manner, pointing out, as he sees it, a kind of eternal truth, as far as poets are concerned, Greek, Egyptian, probably even Babylonian, that "it doesn't change," except that the Reformer collects his salary, but he—Cavafy—does so without rancor and without recourse to monstrosity. Here is the poem in toto:

IN A LARGE GREEK COLONY, 200 B.C.E.

There is not the slightest doubt
that things in the Colony don't go as one would wish,
and though we move forward, anyway,
perhaps, as not a few think, the time has come
for us to bring in a Political Reformer.

Yet the obstacle and difficulty
is that they make a big deal
out of everything, these Reformers.
(It would be a stroke of good luck
if one never needed them.) Everything,
every little thing, they ask about and examine,
and instantly radical reforms come to mind
and they demand they be implemented without delay.

They lean toward sacrifice.
Give up that property of yours,
your owning it is risky:
such possessions are harmful to the Colonies.
Give up that income
and that coming from it,
and this third one, as a natural consequence.
They are essential, but it can't be helped;
They create an adverse liability for you.

And as they proceed in their inspection,
they find (then find again) needless things,

which they demand must go—
things that nevertheless are hard to dismiss.

And when, with good luck, they finish their work,
having ordered and pared everything down to the last detail,
they leave, taking away their rightful wages, as well.
We'll see what remains, after
so much expert surgery.

Perhaps the time had not yet come.
Let's not rush; haste is a dangerous thing.
Premature measures bring regret.
Certainly and unfortunately, there is much disorder in the Colony.
But is there anything human without imperfection?
And, anyway, look, we're moving forward.

[1928]

The last two stanzas are delicious and the penultimate line is the signature supreme. Maybe it's Cavafy's main question "But is there anything human without imperfection?" It may be his homosexuality—and the fact that it was such an omnipresent subject for him—placed him inevitably on the radical edge and even created in him a huge tolerance, an understanding of loneliness, isolation, and suffering, a pity for the despised, for the outcast, and a sympathy for the outsider, Jew, Pagan, Christian, which made it impossible for him to demonize the other, what the politically stupid, thoughtless, or narrow of our time required, artists included. Also he was manifestly good, and sane, and whole, and most of all, kind. Nary a whiff.

Every artist makes a virtue of his weakness—in a way he makes it his subject. Cavafy, overwhelmingly Greek, lived in the diaspora, in a city, Alexandria, that was overwhelmingly mixed, as if it were some Athenian, some Macedonian, backwater, as if a Greek king, minor beyond belief, once reigned there, and he was forgotten, even his name was mispronounced. He lived consciously, deliberately, at a time in the future called the present, where the past was murky, if important. He really had no country, he only had a language. In a way he lived at the end of history, where everything, indeed almost anything, was justified. So he could move easily, and *personally*, from place to place, from century to century, and he could forgive it all, which is what a truly great poet does.

—Gerald Stern
Lambertville, New Jersey

ACKNOWLEDGMENTS

I am lucky that I have family and friends who not only support but are deeply interested in my literary endeavors. Thank you to my community on Serifos, my family, Robert, Deborah, Tony, Sarah, Joseph, Zoë, Alexander, Maya, and the delightful children in the Hurricane Gang (for blowing into another house when I needed to concentrate). Thanks to Anna Grigoriou, Gerard Vollenbrock, Jacoline Vinke and George Papaconstantinou, Michael Kowalski and Elaine Palmer, Costas Meghir and Sophia Skalistiri, Pascal Bonato and Stratos Mastorakis. Katherine Dumas, *merci*. Marianna Cohen, for her clear thoughts about the Greek spellings of names, *Efharisto!* Thanks to Alicia Stallings for inviting me to spread Cavafy's word in a beautiful rooftop reading on Spetses. Thanks so much to friends in America: Christopher Bakken, Tim Fuller, Cynthia Hogue, Alan Michael Parker, Lisa Rhoades, and Mark Turpin. I am grateful to the University of Nevada, Las Vegas, for time to work through course reassignments and a sabbatical. I thank my colleagues at UNLV, especially Chris Hudgins, John Bowers, Evelyn Gajowski, and Wole Soyinka. I thank my students—you know who you are—for their enthusiasm for Cavafy and for their practice of the art of translation. You are the next generation who will bring the world's words to the world. Thank you to everyone at the International Institute of Modern Letters, for promoting translation in the world. Thanks to my friends in the American Literary Translators Association for our shared dream of an enlarged and large-minded community; to John Balaban, Chana Bloch, Khaled Mattawa, Rebecca Seiferle, model poet-translators, and to Robert Hass and Robert Pinsky, early inspiration from my Berkeley days; and to Edwin Honig from my Brown days. My gratitude goes to Martin McKinsey for so many conversations about Cavafy, particularly one that showed me the way to write the introduction to this book. My gratitude goes to Willis for cowriting the notes. Thank you, Gerald Stern, for saying, "I'm the man" to write the preface to this book. My gratitude goes to my editors at W. W. Norton, Jill Bialosky, Evan Carver, and copyeditor David Stanford Burr for their faith, patience, and keen eyes.

I believe that every translation honors those that precede it, so I extend my thanks to all translators of Cavafy, especially to Rae Dalven and to Edmund Keeley and Philip Sherrard.

I would like to thank my mother, Elli Tzalopoulou-Barnstone, for working with me on this book as my native informant and cultural minister, and for checking and double-checking my translations against the Greek to make sure they are correct. I also give her my deep gratitude for her generosity and determination to make her American children Greek. She gave me the motivation and the linguistic help, without which this book is very difficult to imagine.

My sorrowful gratitude goes to my dear friend, the late Cliff Becker (1964–2005), Literature Director of the National Endowment for the Arts. Until his untimely death, Cliff made it his mission to promote translation in the United States, which he did tirelessly, passionately, and effectively. We often spoke of our love of Cavafy. He took particular glee in telling me of seeing Cavafy's house in Alexandria. He enthusiastically wrote me that he couldn't wait to hold this book in his hands. Sadly, he didn't live to see that day, but his spirit dwells in these pages.

Grateful acknowledgment is made to the following journals
in which these translations originally appeared:

The American Poetry Review: "Walls," "An Old Man," "Waiting for
the Barbarians," "Beautiful White Flowers Became Him"
The Blue Moon Review (www.thebluemoon.com): "The Afternoon
Sun," "If Truly Dead"
Colorado Review: "*Che Fece . . . Il Gran Rifiuto*," "On the Ship"
Crab Orchard Review: "The City," "Exiles," "In the Port"
The Drunken Boat (www.thedrunkenboat.com): "Far Off," "When
They Are Aroused," "In the Street," "Days of 1903," "The Next
Table," "In an Old Book—"
Field: "Days of 1909, '10, and '11"
Lyric Poetry Review: Special Issue: Poetry in Times of War: "Antony's
Ending," "Nero's Term," "Of Dimitrios Sotir (162–150 B.C.E.)"
New Letters: "A Byzantine Nobleman in Exile Composing Verses"
Partisan Review: "A Craftsman of Wine Bowls"
Poetry Daily (www.poems.com): "A Craftsman of Wine Bowls"
TriQuarterly: "The Horses of Achilles," "Candles," "King Dimitrios,"
"To Stay"
The Virginia Quarterly Review: "When the Watchman Saw the
Light," "January, 1904," "For the Shop," "Meaning"

INTRODUCTION
C. P. Cavafy: Eros and History as Prophesy

I t was Cavafy's erotic poems that first captivated me. Now I am astonished by the prophesy of his historical poems. I do not mean here to set up a false duality between Cavafy's erotic and historical poems because the two are inseparably connected in his large-minded vision. Cavafy called himself a poet-historian. His work uncannily translates history, the record of the many, into an individual personal document. Though the poet is an external observer of others, the voice of the poetry is that of the observed. His poetry is internal, whether his speaker is a spoiled, rich boy who plans to enter politics or a poor, ostracized, pure, and beautiful young man, destroyed by poverty and priggish social mores; Antony or a poor traveling salesman, who in a rioting crowd hears "the gigantic lie / from the palace—Antony triumphed in Greece." Even when Cavafy is wickedly satirical, as in his portraits of Nero, he takes us deep inside his subject's thought, no matter how delusional or misguided it may be. As such he reminds us that our individual lives are shaped, inevitably, particularly, and sometimes devastatingly, by our historical moment, and, paradoxically, that history is now.

In his own moment of prophesy, W. H. Auden wrote in 1961:

The virtue of patriotism has generally been extolled most loudly and publicly by nations that are in the process of conquering others. . . . To such people, love of one's country involves denying the right of others . . . to love theirs. Moreover, even when a nation is not actively aggressive, the genuineness of its patriotic feelings remains in doubt so long as it is rich, powerful, respected. Will the feeling survive if that nation should become poor and of no political account and aware, also, that its decline is final, that there is no hope for the return of its former glory? In this age, no matter to which country we belong, the future is uncertain enough to make this a real question for us all, and Cavafy's poems more topical than, at first reading, they seem.

Now, as when Auden wrote those words, as when Cavafy wrote his, we are involved in conflicts over resources and which ideology (or theology) will dominate the most minds. I am especially aware of the history of conquest and defeat, of ruin and the desire to regain power, because I was lucky to translate most of the poems in this book on the island of Serifos in the Cyclades. Being in Greece allowed me to understand the poet's spirit of place, though the poetry seems at times willfully (though sorrowfully) to exile itself from location. Though Cavafy's poetry is usually located in Hellenistic or modern Alexandria, Seleucid Asia Minor, or Byzantine Greece, it is so driven by its mytho-historicism that the external landscape is vague. Most often Cavafy's speakers are exiles who long for a place occupied by invaders; the place where they live is not the homeland but the site of alienation. As a result, many of Cavafy's poems are located in a landscape of intimacy: either in the minds of the speakers or inside a room or café. This omission of the details of external location has particular significance for Cavafy's social critiques, which often take the part of young destitute homosexual boys, outsiders who live in a social setting held by hostile forces.

But Serifos is not Alexandria, where Cavafy spent most of his life (though islands do appear in his poems), so how can being on the island unite me with the poet's spirit of place? Let me begin to answer with a poem:

IF TRULY DEAD

"Where has he withdrawn? Where did the Sage disappear?
After his countless miracles,

the fame of his teaching
broadcast in so many nations,
he suddenly hid and no one found out
with certainty what happened
(nor did anyone see his grave).
Some spread a rumor he died in Ephesus.
But Damis did not write it; Damis wrote nothing
about the death of Apollonios.
Others said he vanished in Lindos.
Or is that story
true that he ascended in Crete,
in the ancient temple of Diktynna.—
But still we have his miraculous,
his supernatural apparition
before a young student in Tyana.—
Perhaps the time has not come for him to return,
to show himself to the world again;
but perhaps transfigured
he circulates among us unrecognized.— But he will appear again
as he was, teaching the right path; and, of course, then
he will revive the worship of our gods,
and our refined Greek rituals."

So he dreamed in his shabby house—
after reading Philostratos's
On Apollonios of Tyana—
he, one of the few pagans,
one of the very few remaining. In any case—an insignificant
and timid man—to keep appearances,
he played Christian and he, too, went to church.
It was the era when in utmost piety
old Justin was king,

and Alexandria, god-fearing city,
abhorred miserable idol worshippers.

This is Cavafy the sublime ironist, the wit. I love the sneakiness of this poem. The reader thinks at first that the Sage is Jesus, with his withdrawal, his miracles, his teaching broadcast in nations, and the absence of his grave (parallel to the absence of Jesus's body). Even when we find out that the Sage is Apollonios, we can't shake the association with the Messiah. Perhaps he's "ascended" again; perhaps he's with us now, "transfigured" and "unrecognized." Certainly he will come again "teaching the right path." Then we discover that this is the dream of an outcast and poor pagan, who hopes for a revival of his religion and a restoration of his position, as well. In this poem, as in so many others, Cavafy shows that Christianity is not so far away from the religion it overpowered. The question is which belief system gains dominion, and takes the power and the wealth. The question is who is shunned, and, in order to survive, must keep appearances and behave in ways contrary to his beliefs.

What does this have to do with Serifos? Cycladic civilization is five thousand years old. Every square acre of the craggy mountains is terraced, which means that this mostly barren island was once cultivated and green. Look around and you see ruins, and buildings built upon ruins. The village, Hora, was built on top of a mountain, with gates to the Kastro, the castle, so that when the invaders came—they always came—the Serifiots could barricade themselves there. In the Kastro are three churches built at the highest point. You can see the ancient temple columns in the walls and in the foundations. In the church on the marble-paved square there are columns in the belfry. In the fifteenth-century monastery, in the courtyard, more columns are prominently displayed, like trophies or plunder. On Serifos, as all over Greece, the Christians tore down the temples and used the columns as building materials. I don't need to read a written text to know this history, I can see it every day, living in Hora, just as Cavafy might have seen it:

IONIAN

Because we smashed their statues,
because we threw them out of their temples,
in no way means their gods are dead.
O Ionian land, the gods still love you,
their souls still remember you.
When an August morning dawns over you,
an energy from the gods' lives crosses through your atmosphere;
and sometimes an ethereal adolescent form,
indistinct, with a quick stride,
crosses above your hills.

As this poem indicates, the gods' spiritual presence never left the land vanquished by the Byzantine Empire. And the churches, built with the marble of the temples on the most astonishingly beautiful sites, attest to the sense that the place, rather than the organized religion, was sacred before Christianity. Though it is the conquering faith, Christianity continues the rites of paganism. The Church transforms the pantheon of the gods into the Pantokrator (the Almighty), Mary, Jesus, and the saints. Just as the gods were human, so, too, are the holy ones depicted in the icons, and I have observed the erotic passion with which people kiss their faces. When I go the *panegyria,* the festivals celebrating the saints' days (each at a different church, as if for a different god), I look out over the sea and mountains, knowing there have been sacred rites in this sacred spot for millennia and that we celebrate this anniversary, now called Christian, in much the same way that the pagans did: a ceremony is performed, an animal slaughtered, and we eat, drink island wine, and dance until the sun rises. My mother, who says that Orthodox celebrations are pure Dionysian revelry, likes to tell the story of waking early to pick mountain tea, and finding a *panegyri* still going on, everyone drunk, and the musicians singing, "Penis, penis, penis, vagina, vagina, vagina."

Cavafy's positive relationship to religion, whether pagan or Christian, is sensual, as in the following poem:

ONE OF THEIR GODS

When one of them passed through the agora
of Selefkia around the hour of dusk,
as a tall and perfectly beautiful adolescent
with the joy of his agelessness in his eyes,
with his perfumed black hair,
the passersby looked at him
and asked each other if they knew him,
and asked if he were a Syrian Greek or a stranger. But some,
who looked more carefully, noticed,
understood, and stepped aside;
and as he disappeared under the arches,
among the shadows and light of evening,
headed toward the quarter that lives
only at night, with orgies and riots,
and every kind of intoxication and lewdness,
they mused which of Them he might be
and for which of his suspect pleasures
did he come down to the streets of Selefkia
from the Sacred Worshiped Chambers.

Most of Cavafy's poems dealing with Christianity are satirical, especially those that deal with dogma. When he loves the Church, he loves the physical church, whose heady and opulent atmosphere pleasures him with its visual, auditory, olfactory, and tactile beauties:

IN CHURCH

I love the church—with its sacred banners,
the silver of its vessels, its candelabra,
the lights, its icons, its pulpit.

As I enter the church of the Greeks,
with the fragrance of its incense,
its liturgical voices and harmonies,
the priests' magnificent presence,
their each movement in solemn rhythm,
dazzling in their adorned vestments—
my mind goes to the great honors of our people,
to our glorious Byzantium.

The Church embodies history and transports him to a place that is a sanctuary from the fall of the Byzantine Empire. Despite global defeat, inside the Church, Byzantium reigns glorious. In fact, most Greeks love the Church for the same reasons, not for theology, but for identity and ecstasy; they are taught that church schools carried on Greek language and culture during four and a half centuries of Turkish occupation. (And, sadly, the perception that to be Greek is to be Christian has led, as well, to terrible anti-Semitism. Cavafy's vision of being Greek is not exclusionary, as is revealed in such poems as "If Truly Dead," which criticizes the bigotry of Christian Alexandria.)

In church, and in Cavafy's poetry, history is present and present tense. The past erotically merges with the present, and becomes myth—as ageless as the god passing through the agora in Selefkia. The poet also mythologizes space:

IN THE SAME SPACE

Surroundings of the house, meeting places, neighborhoods
that I see and where I walk, for years and years.

I created you with joys and sorrows,
so many events, so many things.

And you've made yourself all feeling for me.

The "surroundings of the house, meeting places, neighborhoods"
where the poet lives "in the same space" are subject to time; he walks
there "for years and years." He re-creates physical location with emo-
tions and his past, and, in turn, place becomes "all feeling." This is an
erotic relationship because the poet and the place touch each other
with feeling and are transformed.

So often when Cavafy writes about love he simultaneously explores
the power dynamics of ethnic, national, and religious identity. We
hear the inner voices of those who, like us, are involved in a holy war.
(And most wars are holy; even those that, on the surface, are fought
over the national interest must evolve into a sacred and just cause,
otherwise why sacrifice lives?) Here is a pagan young man whose
Christian friend has died:

MYRIS: ALEXANDRIA, 340 C.E.

When I heard the disaster that Myris was dead,
I went to his house, though I avoid
entering Christian houses,
especially when they mourn or celebrate.

I stood in the hall. I didn't want
to go farther inside because I noticed

the relatives of the deceased looking at me
with obvious bewilderment and displeasure.

They had laid him out in a large room
(I could see a bit
from where I stood) full of precious rugs
and vessels made of silver and gold.

I stood and cried in a corner of the hall.
And I thought without Myris
our get-togethers and outings
would no longer be worth anything;
and I thought I'd no longer see him
at our beautiful and lascivious all-night parties,
nor happy, nor laughing, nor reciting verses
with his perfect feel for Greek meter;
and I thought I lost his beauty
forever, I lost forever
the young man I passionately adored.

Some old women near me were talking in low voices
about the last day he lived—
Christ's name was always on his lips;
in his hand he held a cross.
Then four Christian priests
entered the room, ardently saying prayers
and entreating Jesus
or Mary (I don't know their religion well).

Of course, we knew Myris was a Christian.
We knew from the first moment
he joined our group, the year before last.

But he behaved just as we did.
He was the most dissolute of all of us in his pleasures,
lavishly throwing away his money on entertainment.
He was careless about the world's regard;
he threw himself willingly into nighttime street brawls
when it happened that our gang
met a rival one.
He never spoke of his religion.
In fact, one day we told him
we would take him with us to the Serapeion.
But he seemed annoyed
with our joke: I remember now.
Ah, and another two incidents come to mind.
When we made libations to Poseidon,
he withdrew from our circle and looked away.
When one of us said fervently
may our group be
favored and protected by the great
and most beautiful Apollo—Myris whispered
(the others didn't hear), "Except me."

In resounding voices the Christian priests
prayed for the soul of the young man.—
I noticed with how much diligence
and intense concern for the rites
of their religion they prepared
everything for a Christian burial.
And suddenly a strange sensation
took hold of me. Vaguely, I felt
as if Myris were leaving me;
I felt as if he, as a Christian, were joining
his own, and I were becoming

a stranger, a total stranger. I also felt
a doubt seize me: perhaps I was deluded
by my passion, and I was always a stranger to him.—
I flung myself out of their awful house;
I left quickly before the memory of Myris
was snatched away, before their Christianity falsified it.

This poem is characteristic of Cavafy in the way it combines an
individual perspective with political analysis. Because the poem is
utterly personal, the reader is drawn irresistibly inside the conscious-
ness of the speaker, whose narrative delineates the anatomy of alien-
ation and connection, and how connection can degenerate into
hostility, once group doctrine defines it. When the speaker notices
that Myris's relatives look at him with "obvious bewilderment and dis-
pleasure," we feel the dehumanizing effect of sectarian identity when
it erases individual identity. But the speaker, too, cannot relate to the
Christians any more than they can to him. He "adored" Myris and
now he must contend not only with his friend's dying, but the doubt
that their love ever existed: "perhaps I was deluded / by my passion,
and I was always a stranger to him." He wants to preserve the mem-
ory of his beloved, so he flings himself "out of their awful house / . . .
before the memory of Myris / was snatched away, before their
Christianity falsified it." Underlying the narrative is an anger, which
we understand in a primal way—for it is borne of betrayal, jealousy,
and exclusion. We see how such an anger could lead to violence.
Tragically, we also see the Christian Myris depicted by the personal
and specific love of his historical pagan adversary, and this intimate
portrait intensifies the horror of intolerance. Though Cavafy shows
the ways a person's life may be tyrannized and destroyed by labels,
names, custom, and doctrine, he sees the light of the individual,
unobscured by these empty forms.

Through his poetry Cavafy made the figures of the past live, and he created a place for them to live "out of Time," as he says in the poem, "On the Ship." He, like all Greeks, was a spiritual exile from the Polis (or "the City" as Constantinople is called). The translator hopes to end the exile of the foreign text by traveling in imagination, if not physically, to "the same space" as the author and re-creating its "surroundings" with "joys and sorrows." As poet-historian, Cavafy's ecstasy was to put himself in the place of people who dwelled in the past (and of the young men whom he loved in the past). In his poems the exile or the outcast returns to the homeland of the erotic imagination, which not only accepts but embraces the other.

The
COLLECTED
POEMS
of
C. P. CAVAFY

JULIAN AT THE MYSTERIES

When he found himself in the darkness,
in the earth's terrifying depths,
in the company of Greek atheists,
and he saw ethereal shapes come out
before him with glories and bright lights,
the young man was frightened for a moment,
and an instinct returned
from his devout years, and he crossed himself.
Instantly, the Shapes disappeared,
the glories were lost, and the lights went out.
The Greeks exchanged furtive glances.
And the young man said, "Did you see the miracle?
Dear comrades, I'm afraid,
I'm afraid, my friends, I want to leave.
Didn't you see how the demons instantly disappeared
when they saw me make
the holy sign of the cross?"
The Greeks laughed loud with scorn.
"Shame, shame, on you to utter these words
to us, who are sophists and philosophers.
If you want to say such things, say them
to the bishop of Nikomedia and his priests.
The greatest gods of our glorious Greece
appeared before you.
And if they disappeared, don't think for a second
they were afraid of a gesture.
Only when they saw you make
this vile, crude sign,

their noble nature was revolted,
and they left and they disdained you."
So they spoke to him and he turned away
from his sacred and blessed
fear and was convinced
by the godless words of the Greeks.

[1896]

WALLS

Without caution, without pity, without shame
they built thick and high walls around me.

And now I sit here and despair.
I think of nothing else, my mind eaten by this fate

because I had so much to do outside.
Ah, when they built the walls, how did I not notice.

But I never heard the builders or any sound.
Imperceptibly they shut me off from the outside world.

[1897]

AN OLD MAN

In the middle of the noisy café,
hunched over a table, sits an old man,
a newspaper in front of him, with no company.

Wretched with despised old age,
he ponders how little he enjoyed the years
when he had strength and eloquence and beauty.

He knows how much he's aged: he feels it, he sees it.
And yet the time when he was young seems
like yesterday. How brief a time, how brief a time.

And he reflects how Discretion deceived him
and how he always trusted it—what madness!—
he trusted the liar who said, "Tomorrow. You have plenty of time."

He recalls passions he restrained and how much
joy he sacrificed. Now for every lost chance,
he scoffs at his reckless Discretion.

But so much thinking and remembering
has made the old man dizzy. He falls asleep
bent over in the café, on the table.

[1897]

THE HORSES OF ACHILLES

When they saw Patroklos killed,
who was so brave and strong and young,
Achilles' horses began to cry,
their immortal nature outraged
to witness the work of death.
They tossed their heads and waved their long manes,
stamped their hooves on the ground, and they mourned
Patroklos, whom they felt was soulless—ruined—
flesh made lowly now—his spirit lost—
defenseless—without breath—
he had gone from life back to the big Nothing.

Zeus saw the immortal horses' tears
and was sorry. He said, "I should not
have acted so mindlessly at the wedding of Peleus;
it would have been better if we had not given you away,
my unhappy horses! What are you doing down there
with miserable human beings, fate's playthings.
Neither death nor old age pursues you,
yet fleeting disasters torment you.
Men entangled you in their sufferings."
But for the endless disaster of death,
the two noble animals shed their tears.

[1897]

PRAYER

The sea took a sailor into its depths—
His mother, unknowing, goes before the Virgin

and lights a tall candle
for him to come back soon and for good weather—

and always keeps her ear alert to the wind.
But while she prays and entreats her,

the icon listens, grave and sad,
knowing the son she waits for will never return.

[1898]

THE FUNERAL OF SARPEDON

Zeus is heavy with sorrow. Patroklos
killed Sarpedon; and now the son
of Menitiadis and the Achaians rush in
to snatch away and debase his body.

But Zeus doesn't consent at all to such acts.
Beloved boy—whom he let
perish; that was the Law—
at least he will honor him in death.
Look, he sends Apollo down to the plain,
well schooled in how to care for the body.

With reverence and sadness, Apollo raises
the hero's body, and takes it to the river.
He washes away the dust and blood;
closes the wound, not letting
any trace show; pours ambrosial
perfumes on him; and he dresses him
in sparkling Olympian raiment.
He whitens the skin, and with a pearl comb
untangles the jet black hair.
He lays out and arranges the beautiful limbs.

Now he looks like a young charioteer king—
twenty-five or twenty-six years old—
who is resting, after winning the prize in a famous game,
with his all-gold chariot and swiftest horses.

This way Apollo completed his mission,
calling the two brothers, Sleep and Death,
commanding them to take the body
to Lykia, the rich land.

To the rich land, to Lykia,
these two brothers, Sleep and Death, set out on foot,
and when they reached the door of the royal house,
they delivered the glorious body,
and then returned to other cares and tasks.

And when they received the body there in the house,
with processions and honor and dirges
and with abundant libations from sacred wine bowls
and with all that is fitting, the sorrowful burial began.
Then the experienced state craftsmen
and the renowned stone carvers
came and made the tomb and the stele.

[1898]

CANDLES

The days of the future stand before us
like a row of small lighted candles—
golden, warm, and lively candles.

The days of the past stay behind,
a sad line of burned-out candles;
still smoking are the closest ones,
cold candles, melted and drooping.

I don't want to look at them, their aspect saddens me,
and it saddens me to remember their first light.
I look ahead to my lighted candles.

I don't want to look back, to see, horrified,
how quickly the dark line lengthens,
how quickly the snuffed-out candles multiply.

[1899]

THE FIRST STEP

One day the young poet Evmenis
complained to Theokritos,
"I've been writing now for two years
and have composed only one idyll.
It's my only completed work.
Sadly I see the ladder of poetry
reaches high, so very high.
Unhappily for me, I'll never climb higher
than this first step where I stand."
Theokritos said, "Those words
are unseemly and blasphemous.
And if you are even on the first step,
it should make you proud and happy.
You've reached here, no small feat.
Just what you have done is a great glory.
Even this first step
is a long way from ordinary people.
To climb up to this height
you must be in your own right
a citizen in the city of ideas.
And to become a citizen of that city
is difficult and rare.
In its agora you will find Legislators
who won't be duped by charlatans.
You've reached here, no small feat.
just what you have done, a great glory."

[1899]

12

WHEN THE WATCHMAN SAW THE LIGHT

Winter and summer the watchman sat on the roof
of the palace of the sons of Atreus and looked out. Now he tells
the joyful news. He saw a fire flare in the distance.
And he is glad, and his labor is over as well.
It is hard work night and day,
in heat or cold, to look far off
to Arachnaion for a fire. Now the desired
omen has appeared. When happiness
arrives it brings a lesser joy
than expected. Clearly,
we've gained this much: we are saved from hopes
and expectations. Many things will happen
to the Atreus dynasty. One doesn't have to be wise
to surmise this now that the watchman
has seen the light. So, no exaggeration.
The light is good, and those that will come are good.
Their words and deeds are also good.
And we hope all will go well. But
Argos can manage without the Atreus family.
Great houses are not eternal.
Of course, many will have much to say.
We'll listen. But we won't be fooled
by the Indispensable, the Only, the Great.
Some other indispensable, only, and great
is always instantly found.

[1900]

13

THE ENEMIES

Three sophist philosophers came to greet
the consul, who asked them to take their seats
near him; he politely began to speak.
They should take care, he uttered jokingly,
"Fame makes envy. Rivals write. You have enemies."
Then with grave words, replied one of the three:

"Our present enemies will never bring us harm.
Our enemies, new sophists, come later, and alarm
us as we grow old, and are miserably supine, faded,
when some of us will have entered Hades.
Tomorrow, today's words and our works will seem strange
as sophisms, style, and tendencies are changed
by enemies. Similarly, they will be cast
in the same role as we who refashioned the past.
Whatever we have presented as right and beautiful,
the enemies will show is stupid, needless, dull,
while they say the same things differently (without much toil)
just as with new tropes we said words that were old."

[1900]

Translated with Willis Barnstone

CHE FECE . . . IL GRAN RIFIUTO

A day comes to some people when
they must pronounce the great Yes or the great No.
It is instantly clear who has the Yes within,
ready; and by uttering it, he crosses over to

his honor and conviction. The one who
refuses has no remorse. If asked again,
he'd say no again. And yet that No—
the right No—weighs him down to his life's end.

[1901]

Translated with Willis Barnstone

THE SOULS OF OLD MEN

In their ancient time-worn bodies
sit the souls of old men.
How sad those poor souls are
and how bored by the miserable life they endure.
How they tremble to lose life and how they love it,
those confused and contradictory
souls that sit—tragicomic—
inside old decrepit skin.

[1901]

INTERRUPTION

We interrupt the work of the gods,
we the rushed, inexperienced beings of the moment.
In the palaces of Eleusis and Phthia,
Demeter and Thetis begin the ritual of immortality
with great fires and thick smoke. But
always Metaneira rushes out of the king's chambers,
terrified, her hair unbraided,
and fearful Peleus always interferes.

[1901]

THE WINDOWS

In these shadowy rooms where I spend
boring days, I walk back and forth
to find the windows—when a window opens
it will be a consolation.
But the windows are unfindable or I can't find them.
And perhaps it is better not to find them.
Perhaps the light will be a new tyranny. Who knows
what new things it will disclose?

[1903]

Translated with Willis Barnstone

THERMOPYLAE

Honor to those who in their lives
demarcate and guard a Thermopylae.
Never swerving from duty,
just and upright in all their acts,
but compassionate and sad nevertheless;
generous when they are rich, when poor
generous again in small ways,
again rushing to help as much as they can;
always speaking truth
but with no hatred for liars.

And more honor is fitting for them
when they foresee (and many do foresee)
that Efialtis will appear in the end,
and in the end the Medes will break through.

[1903]

GROWING STRONG

He who wishes to strengthen his spirit,
must abandon reverence and submission.
He will honor some laws,
but mostly he will break both law and custom,
and he will stray from the accepted, inadequate straight path.
He will be taught much by sensual pleasures.
He will not fear the destructive act;
half the house must be torn down.
This way he will grow virtuously toward knowledge.

[1903]

SEPTEMBER, 1903

Now at least let me delude myself with lies
so I don't feel my empty life.

And I was so close so many times.
And how paralyzed I was, how cowardly.
Why stay with my lips shut,
so my empty life cries in me
and my desires wear black?

To be so close so many times
to the erotic eyes and lips,
the body I dreamed of and loved.
To be so close so many times.

[1904]

DECEMBER, 1903

And even if I can't speak of my love—
even if I don't speak of your hair, your lips, your eyes,
still your face that I hold in my soul,
the sound of your voice that I hold in my mind,
the days of September that dawn in my dreams,
mold and color my words and my sentences,
no matter what subject I explore, what idea I express.

[1904]

JANUARY, 1904

Ah, these nights of January
when I sit re-creating our moments
in my mind and I meet you
and hear our last words and hear our first.

These desperate nights of January
as vision goes and I am alone.
How does it go, and quickly fade—
gone the trees, gone the streets, gone the houses, gone the lights,
your erotic face erased and lost.

[1904]

ON THE STAIRS

As I went down the sordid stairs,
you were coming through the door, and for an instant
I saw your unfamiliar face and you saw mine.
Then I hid myself so you would not see me again, and you
passed by me quickly, hiding your face,
and slipped into the sordid house,
where you could not have found pleasure, just as I didn't.

And yet the passion you wanted, I possessed to give you;
the pleasure I wanted—your tired and suspicious
eyes told me—you possessed to give me.
Our bodies felt and sought each other;
our blood and skin understood.

But shaken we two hid ourselves.

[1904]

AT THE THEATER

I was bored looking at the stage
and raised my eyes to the boxes.
There in a box I saw you
with your strange beauty and dissolute youth.
All they told me about you this afternoon
came back to mind at once
and aroused my thought and my body.
And as I gazed enthralled
at your weary beauty, your weary youth,
your stylish dress,
I fantasized and pictured you
the way they spoke of you this afternoon.

[1904]

DISLOYALTY

We praise many things in Homer, yet one thing we will not praise . . .
neither will we praise Aeschylus when he makes Thetis say that at her
wedding, Apollo sang the good fortune of her offspring:
> *"that they would not know sickness,*
> *and would live long.*
> *Then he said my fate would be loved by the gods.*
> *He sang a paean that made me joyous.*
> *And I hoped Apollo's divine, unlying mouth,*
> *full of the art of prophesy, would not be false.*
> *He who sang the hymn*
> > *he himself*
> *killed my child."*

—Plato, Republic, II, 383

When they married Thetis to Peleus,
Apollo stood up at the splendid wedding table
and blessed the newlyweds
for the offspring that would come from their union.
He said, "Never will sickness touch him
and he will have long life." As he said this,
Thetis was overjoyed, for Apollo's words,
which she knew from prophecies,
seemed a guarantee for her child.
And as Achilles grew up, and his beauty
was the pride of Thessaly,
Thetis remembered the words of the god.

But one day old men came with news
and told her that Achilles was killed in Troy.
Thetis tore off her purple robes,
and she took off her bracelets and rings
and flung them to the earth.
As she beat her chest, she remembered old things,
and she asked what was wise Apollo doing,
where was he drifting, he who at banquets
speaks so eloquently. Where was the prophet drifting
when they killed her son in the prime of his youth.
And the old men answered it was the same Apollo
who himself descended to Troy,
and with the Trojans killed Achilles.

[1904]

WAITING FOR THE BARBARIANS

—What are we waiting for, gathered in the agora?

    The barbarians are arriving today.

—Why is nothing happening in the Senate?
  Why do the Senators sit making no laws?

    Because the barbarians are arriving today.
    What laws can the Senators make now?
    When the barbarians come, they will make laws.

—Why did our emperor wake up so early,
  and, in the city's grandest gate, sit in state
  on his throne, wearing his crown?

    Because the barbarians are arriving today,
    and the emperor is waiting to receive
    their leader. In fact, he prepared
    a parchment to give them, where
    he wrote down many titles and names.

—Why did our two consuls and the praetors
  come out today in their crimson embroidered togas;
  why did they don bracelets with so many amethysts
  and rings resplendent with glittering emeralds;
  why do they hold precious staffs today,
  beautifully wrought in silver and gold?

Because the barbarians are arriving today,
and such things dazzle barbarians.

—Why don't the worthy orators come as usual
to deliver their speeches and say their piece?

Because the barbarians are arriving today
and they are bored by eloquence and harangues.

—Why should this anxiety and confusion
suddenly begin. (How serious faces have become.)
Why have the streets and squares emptied so quickly,
and why has everyone returned home so pensive?

Because night's fallen and the barbarians have not arrived.
And some people came from the border
and they say the barbarians no longer exist.

Now what will become of us without barbarians?
Those people were some kind of solution.

[1904]

VOICES

Ideal and loved voices
of the dead, or of those
lost to us like the dead.

Sometimes they speak to us in dreams;
sometimes the brain hears them in thought.

And, for one moment, with their sounds,
sounds come back from the first poetry of our lives—
like music at night, remote, fading away.

[1904]

DESIRES

Like beautiful bodies of the dead that haven't aged
and were locked in a brilliant mausoleum with tears,
with roses at their heads and jasmine at their feet,
that is what desires look like when they pass
without having been fulfilled, without even
a single night of passion, or a shining morning

[1904]

Translated with Willis Barnstone

TROJANS

Here are our strivings, we who are doomed.
Here are our strivings like the Trojans'.
We accomplish a bit. We are a bit
encouraged, then we start to feel
brave and raise our hopes high.

But something always comes up and we stop.
Achilles rushes from the trench in front of us
and terrifies us with loud shouts.—

Our strivings are like the Trojans'.
We imagine, if we are determined and bold,
we'll change the course of fate,
and we move out to stand and fight.

But when the great crisis comes,
our determination and boldness disappear,
our souls are shaken, paralyzed,
and we race all around the walls,
trying to save ourselves by fleeing.

Yet our fall is certain. Up there,
within the walls the dirge has already begun.
Memories and feelings cry for our days.
Priamos and Ekavi cry bitterly for us.

[1905]

KING DIMITRIOS

Not like a king but like an actor, he disguised himself
With a brown rather than a tragedian's cloak
And he escaped unnoticed.
                    —Plutarch, *The Life of Dimitrios*

When the Macedonians abandoned him
and showed they preferred Pyrros,
King Dimitrios (who had a great
soul) did not behave—it's said—
at all like a king. He took off
his golden vestments
and threw away his all-crimson
shoes. In humble clothes
he dressed quickly and escaped,
performing just like an actor
who, once the play ends,
changes costume and departs.

[1906]

ANTONY'S ENDING

But when he heard the women weeping—
the lady with her eastern gestures
and her servants with their barbaric Greek
mourning his fall—
the pride of his soul rose up,
his Italian blood was disgusted,
and everything that before he adored blindly
now appeared alien and indifferent—
his whole passionate Alexandrian life—
and he said, "not to cry for him. Such things are not fitting.
Rather they should sing his praises,
for he was a great leader,
and won many riches and much more.
And if he's fallen, he's not fallen humbly,
but as a Roman vanquished by a Roman."

[1907]

THE PROCESSION OF DIONYSOS

Damon the sculptor (there is no better
in all the Peloponnese) carves
the procession of Dionysos
in Parian marble. The god
leads in splendid glory, with powerful strides.
Intemperance follows. Beside Intemperance,
Drunkeness pours the wine for the Satyrs
from an amphora crowned with Ivy.
Close to them is soft Sweetwine,
his eyes half closed, somnolent.
Next come the singers,
Melody and Sweetsong and Reveler, who
never lets the hallowed torch he holds
die out, and next, very modest, is Ritual.—
Damon crafts them all. As he works,
his thought wanders from time to time
to his fee from the king of Syracuse,
three talents, a large sum.
When added to the rest
of his money, he'll live high, prosperous,
and be able to enter politics—joy!—
he, too, will be in the Senate, he, too, in the agora.

[1907]

HIDDEN THINGS

From all I did and all I said
let them not try to find out who I was.
An obstacle stood before me and transformed
my acts and my way of life.
An obstacle stood before me and stopped me
so often from what I was going to say.
My most unnoticed acts
and my most veiled writings—
only from these will they know me.
But maybe it's not worth it to devote
so much care and effort to knowing me.
Later—in a more perfect society—
someone made like me
will certainly appear and act freely.

[1908]

MONOTONY

From one monotonous day, another day
follows, identically monotonous. The same
things will happen. They will happen again.
The same moments find us and leave us.

A month passes and brings in another month.
We easily guess what is to come:
the same boring things from yesterday.
Then tomorrow no longer looks like tomorrow.

[1908]

THIS IS THE MAN

Unknown—a stranger in Antioch—the man from Edessa
writes and writes. And at long last, there, the last
verse is finished. This one makes eighty-three

poems in all. Only the poet
is tired from so much writing, so much versifying,
so much intensity shaping Greek phrases.
And now everything is a burden to him.—

But one thought straight away raises him
from his gloom—the superb "This Is the Man"
Lucian once heard in his sleep.

[1909]

THE FOOTSTEPS

In an ebony bed adorned
with coral eagles, Nero
sleeps deeply—unscrupulous, calm, and happy,
in his prime in his robust flesh,
and exuberant in his beautiful youth.

But in the alabaster hall that holds
the ancient shrine of the Aenobarbi
how uneasy are his Lares.
The small household gods tremble
and try to hide in their insignificant bodies.
Because they've heard an ominous roar,
a deadly roar coming up the stairs,
iron footsteps shaking the stairs.
Faint now, the miserable Lares
withdraw deep into the shrine,
pushing and tripping over each other,
one small god falling over another,
because they understand what kind of a roar this is.
By now they sense the footsteps of the Furies.

[1909]

THE CITY

You said, "I'll go to another land, I'll go to another sea.
I'll find a city better than this one.
My every effort is a written indictment,
and my heart—like someone dead—is buried.
How long will my mind remain in this decaying state.
Wherever I cast my eyes, wherever I look,
I see my life in black ruins here,
where I spent so many years, and ruined and wasted them."

You will not find new lands, you will not find other seas.
The city will follow you. You will roam
the same streets. And you will grow old in the same neighborhood,
and your hair will turn white in the same houses.
You will always arrive in this city. Don't hope for elsewhere—
there is no ship for you, there is no road.
As you have wasted your life here,
in this small corner, so you have ruined it on the whole earth.

[1910]

THE SATRAPY

What bad luck, though you are made
for beautiful and grand works,
your unjust fate always
denies you encouragement and success.
You are hindered by cheap habits
and pettiness and indifference.
And how horrible the day you give in,
(the day you let yourself give in),
when you leave on foot for Susa,
and go to King Artaxerxes,
and he auspiciously gives you a place in his court
and he offers you satrapies and such.
And you accept them in despair,
these things you don't want.
Your soul clamors for other things, weeps for other things:
the praise of the Demos and the Sophists,
the hard won and priceless Cheers,
the Agora, the Theater, and the Laurel Crowns.
How can Artaxerxes give you these,
how can you find them in the satrapy,
and, without them, what life can you lead.

[1910]

41

THE IDES OF MARCH

O soul, fear greatness.
If you can't overcome your ambitions,
follow them with hesitation and caution.
And the more you advance, the more
probing and attentive you must be.

And when you reach your zenith, now a Caesar;
and you take the role of a famous man,
be particularly alert when you go out in the street,
a powerful man in the public eye with an entourage;
if it happens that some Artemidoros from the mob
draws near, bearing a letter,
and says urgently, "Read this at once,
it deals with an important matter concerning you,"
don't fail to pause, don't fail to postpone
any speech or task; don't fail to ward off
those who greet and pay homage to you
(you can see them later); let even the Senate
wait, so you will know right away
the grave writings of Artemidoros.

[1911]

FINISHED

Submerged in fear and suspicion,
with troubled mind and frightened eyes,
we dissolve. We make plans
to avoid the certain danger
so dreadfully threatening us.
But we are mistaken. It does not lie in our path.
The messages were lies
(or we did not hear or heard wrong).
Another catastrophe, never imagined,
sudden, falling in torrents,
finds us unprepared—out of time—and bears us away.

[1911]

A SCULPTOR FROM TYANA

As you may have heard, I'm not a beginner.
Quite a lot of stone has taken shape in my hands.
In my homeland, Tyana, I am well known,
and here senators have commissioned
many statues from me.
                              Let me show you
a few right now. Observe this Rhea,
inspiring reverence, full of fortitude, wholly archaic.
Observe Pompey. Marius,
Paulus Aemilius, Scipio Africanus.
Likenesses faithful as I could make them.
Patroklos (I'll retouch him a bit).
Near the yellowish marble—
those pieces over there—is Kaisarion.

For some time now I've been working on
a Poseidon. I'm particularly studying
his horses, how to form them.
They must be made so light
to show clearly that their bodies, their feet
don't tread on earth, only gallop on water.

But look, here is my work I love most,
made with feeling and greatest care.
With him, on a warm summer day,
when my mind was rising to the ideal,
he came to me in a dream, this young Hermes.

[1911]

44

THE GOD ABANDONS ANTONY

When suddenly at the midnight hour
you hear the invisible troupe passing by
with sublime music, with voices—
don't futilely mourn your luck giving out, your work
collapsing, the designs of your life
that have all proved to be illusions.
As if long prepared, as if full of courage,
say good-bye to her, the Alexandria who is leaving.
Above all don't fool yourself, don't say it was
a dream, how your ears tricked you.
Don't stoop to such empty hopes.
As if long prepared, as if full of courage,
as is right for you who are worthy of such a city,
go stand tall by the window
and listen with feeling, but not
with the pleas and whining of a coward,
and hear the voices—your last pleasure—
the exquisite instruments of that secret troupe,
and say good-bye to her, the Alexandria you are losing.

[1911]
Translated with Willis Barnstone

IONIAN

Because we smashed their statues,
because we threw them out of their temples,
in no way means their gods are dead.
O Ionian land, the gods still love you,
their souls still remember you.
When an August morning dawns over you,
an energy from the gods' lives crosses through your atmosphere;
and sometimes an ethereal adolescent form,
indistinct, with a quick stride,
crosses above your hills.

[1911]

THE GLORY OF THE PTOLEMIES

I am Lagidis, king. The absolute possessor
(with my power and wealth) of pleasure.
No one can be found, neither Macedonian nor barbarian,
who equals me or even comes close. The Selefkid
is laughable with his vulgar hedonism.
If you are searching for something else, look, it is here, clear.
The city Alexandria is teacher, apex of Panhellenism,
and in all fields of knowledge and all the arts, the wisest.

[1911]

ITHAKA

As you set out on the journey to Ithaka,
wish that the way be long,
full of adventures, full of knowledge.
Don't be afraid of Laistrygonians, the Cyclops,
angry Poseidon, you'll never find them on your way
if your thought stays exalted, if a rare
emotion touches your spirit and body.
You won't meet the Laistrygonians
and the Cyclops and wild Poseidon,
if you don't bear them along in your soul,
if your soul doesn't raise them before you.

Wish that the way be long.
May there be many summer mornings
when with such pleasure, such joy
you enter ports seen for the first time;
may you stop in Phoenician emporia
to buy fine merchandise,
mother-of-pearl and coral, amber and ebony,
and every kind of sensual perfume,
buy abundant sensual perfumes, as many as you can.
Travel to many Egyptian cities
to learn and learn from their scholars.

Always keep Ithaka in your mind.
Arriving there is your destination.
But don't hurry the journey at all.
Better if it lasts many years,

and you moor on the island when you are old,
rich with all you have gained along the way,
not expecting Ithaka to make you rich.

Ithaka gave you the beautiful journey.
Without her you would not have set out on your way.
She has no more to give you.

And if you find her poor, Ithaka did not betray you.
With all your wisdom, all your experience,
you understand by now what Ithakas mean.

[1911]

ON HEARING OF LOVE

On hearing of strong love, tremble and be moved
like an aesthete. But, being happy,
remember all those loves your fantasies created for you;
remember these first, then the others—the lesser loves of your life,
the more genuine and palpable, which you experienced and
       enjoyed.
You were not denied such loves.

[1911]

THE DANGERS

Said Myrtias (a Syrian student
in Alexandria during the reign
of Emperor Konstans and Emperor Konstantios;
part pagan, part Christian convert),
"Strengthened with theory and study,
I'm not afraid, like a coward, of my passions.
I will deliver my body to pleasures,
to the leisures of dreams,
to the most daring erotic desires,
to the lustful onrush of my blood, with no
fear at all. For whenever I want,
I will have the will, strengthened
as I'll be with theory and study.
When the decisive moments come, I will find
my spirit again, as it was before, ascetic."

[1911]

PHILHELLENE

Make sure the engraving is done artfully,
the phrasing serious and majestic.
Better that the diadem be rather narrow,
as I don't like those wide ones the Parthians wear.
As usual, make the inscription in Greek,
not hyperbolic, not pompous—
so the proconsul (who's always snooping around
and sending word to Rome) won't take it wrong—
yet even so, naturally, it must bring us honor.
On the other hand, make something utterly exceptional,
a beautiful teenage discus thrower.
Above all, I charge you, take care
(Sithaspis, by God, don't forget this)
that, after the "king" and the "savior,"
"philhellene" is engraved in elegant letters.
Now don't start in with the wisecracks,
like "Where are the Greeks?" and "Where is Greek spoken
here behind the Zagros, beyond Phraata?"
If so many who are so much more barbaric than we
write it, then we can write, too.
Finally, don't forget that from time to time
sophists do come to us from Syria,
and versifiers, and other pseudo-intellectuals.
So we are not un-Hellenized, I believe.

[1912]

HERODIS ATTIKOS

Oh, what glory is this given to Herodis Attikos.

Alexandros of Selefkia, one of our fine sophists,
arrived in Athens to speak
and found the city empty because Herodis
was in his country home. All the young people
had followed him there to hear him.
So the sophist Alexandros writes
a letter to Herodis and entreats him
to send back the Greeks.
At once, the tactful Herodis replies,
"I'm coming, too, along with the Greeks."

How many youths now in Alexandria,
Antioch, or Beirut
(tomorrow's orators whom Hellenism prepares)
gathered at elite banquets,
where at times the talk is about beautiful sophistry
and at times about their exquisite erotic life,
are suddenly distracted and silent.
They leave the glasses before them untouched,
and meditate on the luck of Herodis—
Is another sophist so revered?
Wherever he wants and whatever he does,
the Greeks (the Greeks!) follow him
not to judge or debate,
no longer even to choose. Only to follow.

[1912]

ALEXANDRIAN KINGS

The Alexandrians are gathered together
to see Kleopatra's children,
Kaisarion and his younger brothers,
Alexandros and Ptolemaios, whom they lead
out to the Gymnasium for the first time,
there to proclaim them kings
before a splendid procession of soldiers.

Alexandros—they proclaim him king
of Armenia, Media, and the Parthians.
Ptolemaios—they proclaim him king
of Cilicia, Syria, and Phoenicia.
Kaisarion stood in front,
clothed in rose-colored silk,
at his chest a bouquet of hyacinths,
his belt, a double row of sapphires and amethysts,
his shoes tied with white ribbons,
embroidered with pink pearls.
It was he they proclaimed greater than the younger ones,
it was he they proclaimed the king of kings.
The Alexandrians, of course, felt
this was words and theater.

But the day was warm and poetic,
the sky a light azure,
the Alexandrian Gymnasium
a triumphant work of art,
with courtiers wearing their luxurious best,

Kaisarion all grace and beauty
(son of Kleopatra, blood of the Lagidis dynasty).
And the Alexandrians thronged to the celebration,
enthusiastic and cheering
in Greek and Egyptian and some in Hebrew,
charmed by the beautiful spectacle—
though they knew, of course, what it all was worth,
what hollow words were these kingdoms.

[1912]

COME BACK

Come back often and take me,
beloved sensation, come back and take me—
when my body's memory wakes up
and an old desire courses through the blood again,
when lips and skin remember
and feel hands as if they touched again.

Come back often and take me at night
when lips and skin remember. . . .

[1912]

IN CHURCH

I love the church—with its sacred banners,
the silver of its vessels, its candelabra,
the lights, its icons, its pulpit.

As I enter the church of the Greeks,
with the fragrance of its incense,
its liturgical voices and harmonies,
the priests' magnificent presence,
their each movement in solemn rhythm,
dazzling in their adorned vestments—
my mind goes to the great honors of our people,
to our glorious Byzantium.

[1912]

VERY RARELY

He is an old man. Exhausted and bent,
ravaged by the years and excess,
he walks the narrow street, stepping slowly.
And yet as he enters his house to hide
his wretchedness and old age, he ponders
the share he still has of youth.

Now the young recite his lines.
They see his vision through their lively eyes.
Their sensual, sound minds
and lithe, firm flesh
are moved by his own expression of the beautiful.

[1913]

AS MUCH AS YOU CAN

Even if you can't make your life as you want it,
at least try
as much as you can: don't cheapen it
with too much contact with the world,
with too much activity and talk.

Don't cheapen it, taking it around,
constantly making the rounds, exposing it
to socializing and parties,
the daily nonsense,
until it becomes an alien burden.

[1913]

FOR THE SHOP

He wrapped them carefully and tidily
in precious green silk.

Roses of rubies, lilies of pearl,
violets of amethyst. He judges them

as he wants them to be, sees them beautiful, not as he saw them
in nature, not as he studied them. He will leave them in the safe

as a token of his daring and skilled work.
If some customer comes into the shop,

he takes other things to sell from the cases—first-rate ornaments—
bracelets, chains, necklaces, and rings.

[1913]

I WENT

I did not restrain myself.
I let go completely and I went.
I went in the light-filled night
to pleasures half real,
half turning in my mind.
And I drank strong wines, the same
drunk by brave hedonists.

[1913]

"I WILL TELL THE REST TO THOSE DOWN IN HADES"

"Truly," said the proconsul, shutting the book, "This
verse is beautiful and very correct;
Sophocles wrote it philosophizing deeply.
How many things we'll say there, how many things we'll say there,
and how different we will appear.
These things we guard here like sleepless sentinels,
the wounds and secrets we shut inside ourselves
with heavy daily agony,
there we'll say freely and clearly."

"You might add," said the sophist, half smiling,
"if they say such things in Hades, do they care?"

[1913]

LIKE THIS

In this obscene photograph, which was secretly
sold in the street (so the police would not see),
in this pornographic photograph,
how was such a face
from dreams found, how did you find yourself here?

Who knows the degrading, cheap life you are leading;
how terrible the surroundings
when you posed for them to photograph you;
what a base soul you must have.
But despite this and more, for me you remain
the face from dreams, the form
created for and given to Greek sensuality—
you remain like this for me and like this my poetry names you.

[1913]

EXILES

It is always Alexandria. You walk a bit
down the straight road that ends at the Hippodrome
and you'll see palaces and monuments that awe you.
No matter how much damage it has suffered in wars,
no matter how diminished, it is always a wonderful city.
And then with excursions and books,
and various studies, time passes.
Evenings we gather by the sea,
we five (all, naturally,
with fictitious names) and some other Greeks,
some of the few left in the city.
Sometimes we talk about the church (they seem
somewhat Roman here), sometimes about literature.
The other day we were reading the verse of Nonnos.
What images, what rhythms, what language, what harmony.
We admired the Panopolitan with great enthusiasm.
So the days pass, and our stay here
is not unpleasant because it is understood
that we won't be here forever.
We've heard good news, and whether
something happens in Smyrna now, or whether in April
our friends start out from Epirus, our plans
will succeed, and we will topple Vassilios easily.
And then finally it will be our turn.

[1914]

THE TOMB OF LYSIAS THE GRAMMARIAN

On the right, just as you enter the Beirut library
we buried the learned Lysias the grammarian.
The spot is beautifully apt. We put him close
to the things he remembers even there, perhaps:
his annotations, texts, grammars, scriptures,
a many-volumed series analyzing Greek idioms.
And this way, too, we will see and honor
his tomb when we pass by the books.

[1914]

THE TOMB OF EVRION

In this ornate monument,
made entirely of syenite stone,
covered with so many violets, so many lilies,
beautiful Evrion is buried.
Child of Alexandria, twenty-five years old.
His father was from an old line of Macedonians,
his mother from a line of magistrates.
He was a student of philosophy with Aristokleitos
and of rhetoric with Paros. In Thebes he studied
the sacred texts. He wrote the history
of the province of Arsinoites. At least this will last.
But we lost the most precious. His form
was like a vision of Apollo.

[1914]

CHANDELIER

In an empty and small room, only four walls
covered in deep green cloth,
a beautiful chandelier burns and flares hot,
and in each of its flames blazes
a lusty passion, a lusty impulse.

In the small room brilliantly lighted
by the chandelier's strong flame,
the fire burning is not at all ordinary.
Since timid bodies are not made
for the pleasure of this heat.

[1914]

FAR OFF

I want to speak this memory . . .
But it's erased . . . as if nothing remains—
because it lies far off in my first adolescent years.

Skin as if made of jasmine . . .
That time in August—Was it August?—evening . . .
I scarcely remember those eyes: they were deep blue, I think . . .
Ah, yes, deep blue, a sapphire blue.

[1914]

THE WISE SENSE WHAT IS TO COME

So the gods know the future, people know the present,
the wise sense what is to come.
  Philostratos, *Words of Apollonios of Tyana,* VIII, 7

The people know the present.
The future is known by the gods,
the only and absolute keepers of all the lights.
Of the future, the wise sense
what is to come. Sometimes

in hours of serious study, their hearing
is disturbed. The secret roaring
of coming events reaches them.
And they listen reverently. While in the street
outside, the people hear nothing at all.

[1915]

THEODOTOS

If you are one of the truly elect,
look to how you gain your ascendancy.
No matter how glorified you are,
no matter how loudly the cities hail you
for your feats in Italy and Thessaly,
no matter how many decrees in your honor
your admirers have issued in Rome,
neither your joy nor your triumph will last,
nor will you feel a superior man—how are you superior?—
when in Alexandria, Theodotos brings you
the head of miserable Pompey
on a bloody tray.

And do not rest assured that your life,
which is confined, orderly, and prosaic,
does not hold such spectacle and dread.
Perhaps at this hour inside
one of your neighbor's well-kept homes,
Theodotos enters—invisible, bodiless—
carrying one such ghastly head.

[1915]

70

AT THE CAFÉ DOOR

Something those next to me said
turned my attention to the café door.
And I saw the beautiful body that seems
as if Eros made it with his supreme experience—
molding his symmetrical limbs with joy,
erecting his statuesque height,
molding his face with emotion,
and with a touch of his hands, leaving
a feeling on his forehead, eyes, and lips.

[1915]

HE SWEARS

He swears every so often   to start a better life.
But when night comes   with its own advice,
its compromises,   and its promises—
but when night comes   with its own power
over the body that wants and demands,
he goes back, lost, to the same fatal joy.

[1915]

AS I LOUNGED AND LAY ON THEIR BEDS

When I entered the house of pleasure,
I did not stay in the front rooms where they celebrated
conventional lovemaking with some order.

I went to the secret rooms
and I touched and lay down on their beds.

I went to the secret rooms
they considered shameful even to name.
But not shameful to me—because then
what kind of poet and craftsman would I be?
Better to be a hermit. It would be more in keeping,
much more in keeping with my poetry,
than to take my pleasure in the commonplace rooms.

[1915]

ONE NIGHT

The room was shabby and cheap,
hidden above the suspect taverna.
The window looked out on the alley,
filthy and narrow. From below
came voices of some workers
playing cards and partying.

And there on the common, humble bed
I had love's body, I had those lips,
inebriating, sensual, like roses,
their rosiness so transporting that now
as I write—after so many years!
in my lonely house, I'm drunk again.

[1915]

MORNING SEA

Let me stop here. Let me, too, look at nature awhile.
The glowing blue of the morning sea
and cloudless sky and yellow shore, all
beautiful and brightly lighted.

Let me stop here. Let me pretend I see all this
(I really did see it for a second when I first stopped)
and not here, too, the usual daydreams,
my memories, the images of the body's pleasure.

[1915]
Translated with Willis Barnstone

DRAWN

I'm attentive to my work and I love it.
But today how slowly I compose discourages me.
The day has affected me. Its whole face
darkens. All wind and rain.
I'd much rather see than speak.
In that picture I see now
a beautiful boy who lay
beside the fountain, tired of running.
What a lovely child; what a divine noon
took him to sleep.
I sit gazing like this a long time.
And I'm inside my art again, where working rests me.

[1915]

OROFERNIS

He who is on the four-drachma coin
whose face looks as if it's smiling,
this beautiful, delicate face,
this is Orofernis, son of Ariarathis.

As a child they threw him out of Cappadocia,
out of the grand ancestral palace,
and they sent him off to grow up
in Ionia, to be forgotten among strangers.

Ah, exquisite Ionian nights
when fearless, and in an utterly Greek way,
he fully knew pleasure.
In his heart always Asian,
but in his manner and speech Greek,
adorned in turquoise, in Greek dress,
his body fragrant with jasmine perfume,
of all the beautiful young men of Ionia,
he was the most beautiful, the ideal.

Later when the Syrians entered Cappadocia
and made him king,
he immersed himself in his monarchy
so he could enjoy himself in a new way each day,
so he could greedily amass gold and silver,
and revel and boast,
seeing around him piles of shining riches.

As for caring for the country or ruling it—
he didn't know what was happening around him.

The Cappadocians soon deposed him,
and he wound up in Syria, in the palace
of Dimitrios where he lazed around, amusing himself.

Yet one day unusual thoughts
interrupted his great sloth.
He recollected that by his mother Antiohida,
and by that ancient Stratoniki,
he, too, was descended from the Syrian crown,
and he was almost a Selefkid.
For a little while he emerged
from his lust and drunkeness
and ineffectually and half dazed,
tried to create an intrigue,
to do something, to plot something,
and he failed miserably and was destroyed.

His end must have been written someplace and lost,
or perhaps history passed it by
and, justly, did not deign to make a note
of such an insignificant event.

He who is on the four-drachma coin
left a grace from his beautiful youth,

a light from his poetic beauty,
an aesthetic memory of an Ionian boy.
This is Orofernis, son of Ariarathis.

[1916]

THE BATTLE OF MAGNESIA

He's lost his old verve, his courage.
He will attend mainly to his body, so worn out now,

it's almost ill. And the rest of his life will pass
carefree. This is what Philip claims, anyway.

Tonight he is throwing dice.
He's inclined to amuse himself.

Arrange countless roses on the table. And what if
Antiohos was vanquished in Magnesia.

They say scores of his brilliant army were massacred.
Maybe they exaggerate; it can't all be true.

Let's hope. Because, though the enemy, they are our tribe.
But one "Let's hope" is enough. Maybe too much.

Of course, Philip won't put off the festivities.
No matter how deeply weary of life he has ended up,

he's held onto one good thing. His memory
doesn't leave him at all. He remembers

how much they mourned in Syria,
the kind of sorrow they felt

when their mother Macedonia was turned to trash.
Let the banquet begin. Slaves! the flutes, the lights.

[1916]

MANUEL KOMNINOS

On a melancholy September day,
the Lord King Manuel Komninos
feels his death is near. The court astrologers
(who are paid) chatter
about how many more years he will live.
But while they talk, the king
remembers a pious old custom,
and orders ecclesiastic vestments
brought to him from the monastery cells,
and he wears them, glad he evinces
the modest aspect of a priest or a monk.

Happy are all those who believe
and, like the Lord King Manuel, end their lives
so humbly dressed in their faith.

[1916]

THE DISPLEASURE OF THE SELEFKID

Dimitrios the Selefkid was displeased
to learn a Ptolemy arrived in Italy,
in such a wretched state,
with only three or four slaves,
poorly dressed and on foot. What an irony
to fall so low, and for their dynasty
to become a joke in Rome. The bottom line
is they've become something like servants
to the Romans. The Selefkid knows it.
The Romans grant them their thrones
capriciously, just as they please. He knows that, too.
But at least in their appearance
let them keep some magnificence,
let them not forget that they are still kings,
that they still (alas!) are called kings.

This is why Dimitrios the Selefkid was distressed,
and he immediately offered the Ptolemy
purple raiment, a dazzling crown,
precious gems, many
servants and attendants, and his costliest horses,
so he could present himself to Rome properly,
as an Alexandrian Greek monarch.

But Lagidis, the Ptolemy who came to supplicate,
knew his business and refused it all;
he had no need whatsoever for these luxuries.
Shabbily dressed, humbled, he entered Rome

and stayed in the home of a minor craftsman.
Then he appeared wretched
and poverty-stricken before the Senate
so he could more effectively beg.

[1916]

WHEN THEY ARE AROUSED

Try to keep them, poet—
no matter how few are stilled—
those visions of your eroticism.
Put them, half hidden, in your sentences.
try to keep them, poet,
when they are aroused in your mind
at night or in the brilliance of noon.

[1916]

IN THE STREET

His amiable face, a bit pale;
his eyes, a bit glazed;
twenty-five years old but he looks twenty.
With something artistic in his dress
—something about the color of his tie and the shape of his collar—
he wanders aimlessly in the street
as if still hypnotized by the illicit pleasure,
the intensely illicit pleasure he had.

[1916]

BEFORE THE STATUE OF ENDYMION

On a white chariot pulled by four
all-white mules adorned with silver,
I arrived in Latmon from Miletos. To perform
the sacred rites—sacrifices and libations—to honor Endymion,
I came by sea from Alexandria on a crimson trireme.—
Here is the statue. Now in ecstasy I see
the celebrated beauty of Endymion.
My servants empty baskets of jasmine;
those auspicious tributes awaken the pleasure of ancient times.

[1916]

IN A CITY OF OSROINI

After the fight in the taverna, yesterday around midnight,
they brought us our wounded friend Remon.
From the window we left wide open, the moon spread light
over his beautiful body on the bed. We are a blend
here: Syrians, Greeks, Armenians, Medes.
So is Remon. But yesterday, when the moon illuminated
his erotic face, our minds turned to Plato's Charmides.

[1917]

PASSING THROUGH

Things he imagined shyly as a student are open,
revealed before him. And he roams about, stays up all night,
and is swept away. As is right (for our art),
pleasure itself enjoys
his blood, new and hot. Illicit erotic drunkenness
overcomes his body, and his young limbs
give in to it.
      And in this way a simple young man
becomes worth our watching; and from the High
World of Poetry for an instant he, too, passes through—
the sensual young man, his blood new and hot.

[1917]

FOR AMMONIS, WHO DIED AT TWENTY-NINE, IN 610

Raphael, they ask for you to compose some lines
for the epitaph of the poet Ammonis.
Something very refined and polished. You can do it.
You're the proper one to write as befits
the poet Ammonis, our very own.

Of course, you will discuss his poems—
but talk about his beauty, too,
the delicate beauty we loved.

Your Greek is always beautiful and musical,
yet now we need all your craft.
Our love and sorrow pass into a foreign tongue.
Pour your Egyptian feeling into the foreign tongue.

Raphael, your verses should be written
so—you know—they embody something of our lives,
so the rhythm and each phrase proclaim
that an Alexandrian is writing for an Alexandrian.

[1917]

ONE OF THEIR GODS

When one of them passed through the agora
of Selefkia, around the hour of dusk,
as a tall and perfectly beautiful adolescent
with the joy of his agelessness in his eyes,
with his perfumed black hair,
the passersby looked at him
and asked each other if they knew him,
and asked if he were a Syrian Greek or a stranger. But some,
who looked more carefully, noticed,
understood, and stepped aside;
and as he disappeared under the arches,
among the shadows and light of evening,
headed toward the quarter that lives
only at night, with orgies and riots,
and every kind of intoxication and lewdness,
they mused which of Them he might be
and for which of his suspect pleasures
did he come down to the streets of Selefkia
from the Sacred Worshiped Chambers.

[1917]

EVENING

Anyway, they would not have lasted long. So the experience
of the years shows me. But Fate came
somewhat hastily and stopped them.
The good life was short.
But how strong the perfumes were,
how divine the beds where we lay,
to what pleasure we gave our bodies.

An echo of the days of pleasure,
an echo of the days came close to me,
something of our youth's fire, something of the two of us.
In my hands was a letter I picked up again,
and I read it again and again until the light was gone.

I went out on the balcony, melancholy—
I went out to change my thoughts, at least to see
a little of the beloved city,
a little of the activity in the streets and the stores.

[1917]

SENSUAL PLEASURE

Joy and perfume of my life—the memory of the hours
when I found and held sensual pleasure as I wanted it.
Joy and perfume of my own life—because I turned away revolted
from enjoying any routine erotic love.

[1917]

GRAY

Looking at a half-gray opal
I remembered two beautiful gray eyes
I saw. It must be twenty years ago . . .

* * *

We loved each other a month.
Then he left for Smyrna, I think,
to work there, and we never saw each other again.

They must have grown ugly—if he is alive—the gray eyes.
The beautiful face must be ruined.

Memory, keep them as they were.
Memory, bring back whatever you can of my passion,
bring back to me whatever you can tonight.

[1917]

THE TOMB OF IASIS

I, Iasis, lie here. In this great city,
the young man most renowned for beauty.
Profound wise men admired me, also superficial
simple people. And I took joy in both equally.

But because the people held me up as Narcissus or Hermes,
the excesses wore me out, killed me. Passerby,
if you are from Alexandria, you won't condemn me. You know our life's
onrush, what heat, what supreme pleasure.

[1917]

IN THE MONTH OF ATHYR

With difficulty I read   on the ancient stone
"Lo[r]d Jesus Christ."   I make out one "s[o]ul."
"In the month of Athyr"   "Lefkio[s] went to sleep."
In noting his age   "he li[ve]d from the years,"
the Kappa Zeta show   he died young.
In the eroded letters I see   "H[im] . . . Alexandrian."
Then are three lines   badly defaced,
but I make out some words—   like "our t[e]ars," "sorrow,"
and again "tears,"   and "t[o u]s his mourning [f]riends."
To me it seems Lefkios   was beloved.
In the month of Athyr   Lefkios went to sleep.

[1917]

I HAVE GAZED SO LONG—

I have gazed at beauty so long,
my vision is filled with it.

Lines of the body. Red lips. Sensual limbs.
Hair as if taken from Greek statues,
always beautiful, even if unkempt,
and falling, a little, on white foreheads.
Faces of love, just as my poetry
wanted them . . . in the nights of my youth,
in my nights, in secret, found.

[1917]

THE TOMB OF IGNATIOS

Here I am not Kleon, famous
in Alexandria (where they are difficult to impress)
for my splendid houses and gardens,
horses and carriages,
the jewelry and silks I wore.
All gone. Here I am not that Kleon,
his twenty-eight years to be erased.
I am Ignatios, a reader, who very late
came to my senses; nonetheless, for ten months I lived happy
in the serenity and safety of Christ.

[1917]

HOUSE WITH GARDEN

I'd like a country house
with a very large garden—not so much
for the flowers, trees, and greenery
(of course, I'd have them, too—they're lovely)
but to have animals. Ah, to have animals!
At least seven cats—two jet black
and two snow white, for contrast.
An outstanding parakeet, to listen to him
speak emphatically, with conviction.
As for dogs, I believe three would be enough.
I'd like two horses (how good little horses are).
And for sure, three or four of those distinguished,
amiable animals, donkeys,
to keep them idle, their big heads joyful.

[1917]

DAYS OF 1903

I've not found them again—so swiftly lost . . .
the poetic eyes, the pale
face . . . the night lengthening into the street . . .

I've not found them again—all possessed wholly by chance—
I so easily cast them aside
then later, anguished, wanted them.
The poetic eyes, the pale face,
the lips I never found again.

[1917]

HALF AN HOUR

I never possessed you, nor will I
ever, I believe. A few words, a drawing near,
as in the bar the other day, and nothing more.
I can't say it's not a pity. But we who belong to the Art
create with the mind's intensity
a sensuality that seems almost physical—
only for a short time, of course.
So in the bar the other day—helped a lot
by compassionate alcoholism—
I had a perfect erotic half an hour.
And I believe you understood,
and stayed a little longer on purpose.
It was very necessary. Because
with all the imagining and the magic alcohol,
I needed to look at your lips;
I needed your body close by.

[1917]

THE TOBACCO SHOP WINDOW

Near a well-lighted tobacco shop
window, he was standing among many others.
By chance their gazes met,
and they warily, hestitantly
expressed the illicit desires of their flesh.
Then a few anxious steps on the pavement—
until they smiled and nodded slightly.

Then, of course, the closed carriage . . .
the sensual closeness of their bodies,
the joined hands, the joined lips.

[1917]

REMEMBER, BODY...

Body, remember not only how much you were loved,
not only the beds where you lay,
but also those desires for you,
shining clearly in eyes
and trembling in a voice—and some chance
obstacle thwarted them.
Now when everything is the past,
it almost looks as if you gave yourself
to those desires as well—how they shone—
remember—in the eyes that looked at you,
how they trembled for you in the voice—remember, body.

[1917 or 1918]

THE TOMB OF LANIS

The Lanis you loved isn't here, Markos,
in the tomb where you come and cry, and stay hours and hours.
The Lanis you loved is closer to you
when you shut yourself in your house and look at the painting
that somehow preserved what was precious in him,
that somehow preserved what you loved in him.

Remember, Markos, when you brought the famous
Kyrenian painter from the proconsul's palace,
and with what artistic cunning
the instant he saw your friend he wanted to convince you
he absolutely must make him look like Hyacinth
(this way his painting would be more renowned).

But your Lanis would not lend his beauty like that,
and firmly resisted him, saying not to depict
Hyacinth or anyone else,
but Lanis, son of Rametihos, an Alexandrian.

[1917 or 1918]

MEANING

The years of my youth, my sensual life—
how clearly I see their meaning now.

What needless repentances, how futile . . .

But I didn't see the meaning then.

Out of the dissolute life of my youth
my poetry's aims grew,
my art's realm was drawn.

That is why the repentances were never steadfast.
And my resolutions to hold back, to change,
lasted two weeks at most.

[1917 or 1918]

KAISARION

In part to verify an era,
in part to pass the time,
last night I chose a collection
of Ptolemaic epigraphs to read.
The extravagant praise and flattery
was the same for everybody. All are splendid,
glorious, powerful, and altruistic;
every undertaking very wise.
If you talk about the women of that generation, they, too,
all the Berenikis and Kleopatras, were marvelous.

When I succeeded in verifying the era,
I would have put the book down if a small
and unimportant note about King Kaisarion
did not immediately attract my attention.

Ah, here you came with your ambiguous
charm. In history only a few
lines about you exist,
and so I created you more freely in my mind.
I created you handsome and sensitive.
My art gives your face
a dreamy, amiable beauty.

And I imagine you so fully
that late last night as my light
went out—I let it go out on purpose—
I imagined you came in my room,

it seemed to me you stood as before, as you would have
in the vanquished Alexandria,
pale and tired, ideal in your sorrow,
still hoping they might show you compassion,
the vicious ones—who whispered, "too many Caesars."

[1918]

NERO'S TERM

When Nero heard the prophesy of the Delphic Oracle
he wasn't worried.
"Fear the seventy-three years."
He still had time to enjoy himself.
He is thirty years old. The term the god
has given him is more than enough
to take care of future dangers.

Now he will return to Rome a little tired,
yet delightfully tired from this trip
given fully to days of pleasure—
in the theaters, the gardens, the athletic fields . . .
evenings in the Achaian cities . . .
Ah, the pleasure of the naked bodies, most of all.

So Nero thought. And in Spain, Galba
secretly rallies and drills his army,
that old man of seventy-three.

[1918]

108

ENVOYS FROM ALEXANDRIA

For centuries they have not seen such beautiful gifts in Delphi
as these sent by the two brothers,
the rival Ptolemaic kings. Yet after they received them,
the priests grow uneasy about the oracle. They will need
all their experience to compose it shrewdly—
which one, which one of such a pair, to displease?
And they confer secretly at night
and discuss the affairs of the Lagidis family.

But look, the envoys are back. They say their good-byes.
They're returning to Alexandria, they say. And they don't seek
any oracle at all. The priests hear this with delight
(it's understood they'll keep the marvelous gifts),
yet they are also totally mystified,
not comprehending what this sudden indifference means.
They're unaware that yesterday the envoys received grave news.
The oracle was pronounced in Rome.
They allotted the kingdoms there.

[1918]

ARISTOVOULOS

The palace weeps, the king weeps,
King Herod mourns inconsolably,
the whole city weeps for Aristovoulos,
who so senselessly drowned by chance,
playing with his friends in the water.

And when they learn the news in other places,
when it spreads up to Syria,
even among the Greeks, many will be saddened
and the poets and sculptors will grieve
because they have heard of this Aristovoulos,
and never have their fantasies of an adolescent
equaled the beauty of this boy.
And could Antioch claim a statue of a god
like this child of Israel?

The First Princess, his mother,
the greatest Jewish woman, wails and weeps.
Alexandra wails and weeps for the calamity.
But when she finds herself alone her sorrow changes.
She moans, rages, reviles, curses.
How they tricked her! How they deceived her!
How they finally achieved their goal.
They destroyed the house of the Hasmoneans.
How did this criminal king pull it off,
the schemer, the villain, the scoundrel?
How did he pull it off? What a diabolical plot
so even Miriam didn't notice a thing.

If Miriam had noticed anything, if she'd suspected,
she would have found a way to save her brother—
she's a queen, after all, and would have done something.
How they must be triumphing now and secretly glad,
those vicious women, Kypros and Salome,
those vulgar women, Kypros and Salome—
and to be powerless and forced
to pretend she believes their lies,
not to be able to go to the people,
to go out and to shout to the Jews,
to tell, to tell how the murder was committed.

[1918]

IN THE PORT

Young, twenty-eight years old, on a boat from Tinos
Emis arrived in this Syrian port—to learn
to make perfume was his goal. But he fell ill
on the journey and died as soon as he landed.
His burial took place here, among the poorest of the poor.
A few hours before he died, he murmured
something about "home" and "very old parents."
But who they were, no one knew, nor
where his homeland was in the great Panhellenic world.
It's better. For this way, while he lies dead in this port,
his parents will always hold out hope he is alive.

[1918]

AIMILIANOS MONAI, ALEXANDRIAN, 628-655 C.E.

With words, appearance, and manners
I will create an extraordinary armor;
and this way I will face evil men
with no fear or weakness.

They will want to harm me, but none
who come near will know
where my wounds, my weak spots, lie
under my lies protecting me.—

Boastful rhetoric of Aimilianos Monai.
I wonder if he ever made that armor?
In any case, he didn't wear it long.
At twenty-seven he died in Sicily.

[1918]

SINCE NINE O'CLOCK—

Twelve-thirty. Time passes quickly
since nine o'clock when I lit the lamp
and sat down here. I've been sitting here, not reading,
not speaking. Whom could I speak to
all alone in the house?

Since nine o'clock when I lit the lamp
the image of my young body
came and reminded me
of closed, perfumed rooms
and past pleasure—what daring pleasure!
And it also brought before my eyes
streets that now are unrecognizable,
nightclubs full of life, now closed,
and theaters and cafés that used to be.

The image of my young body
came and brought me sorrows as well:
family mourning, separations,
feelings of my kin, little appreciated feelings
of the dead.

Twelve-thirty. How quickly time passes.
Twelve-thirty. How quickly the years pass.

[1918]

114

OUTSIDE THE HOUSE

Yesterday walking in an outlying
neighborhood, I passed by the house
where I went when I was very young.
There Eros received my body
with his exquisite power.
                          And yesterday
as I passed by on the old road,
suddenly the charm of love made everything beautiful,
the shops, the sidewalks, stones,
and walls and balconies and windows;
nothing ugly remained there.

And as I stood looking at the door,
and as I stood lingering outside the house,
my whole being emanated
pent-up sensual feeling.

[1919]

THE NEXT TABLE

He must be barely twenty-three years old.
And yet I am sure almost as many
years ago, I enjoyed this same body.

It isn't merely an erotic flush.
I've only been in the casino a little while
and haven't even had time to drink a lot.
I enjoyed this same body.

And even if I don't recall where—one lapse of memory means nothing.

Ah, now, there, now that he sits at the next table,
I know each way he moves—and under his clothes,
naked, are the loved limbs I see again.

[1919]

THE BANDAGED SHOULDER

He said he banged it against a wall or he fell.
But perhaps there was another reason
for the wounded and bandaged shoulder.

When he moved a bit roughly
to take down from a shelf
a few photographs he wanted to look at more closely,
the bandage came undone and some blood dripped.

I rewrapped the shoulder and, as I wrapped,
went rather slowly, since he was not in pain,
and I liked looking at the blood. The blood
was part of my pleasure.

After he left, in front of the chair, I found
a blood-stained rag from the dressing,
a rag ready to go straight into the garbage,
and I brought it to my lips
and held it there a long time,
the blood of love on my lips.

[1919]

THE AFTERNOON SUN

This room, how well I know it.
Now they rent it and the one next door
as commercial offices. The whole house became
offices for agents and merchants and companies.

Ah, this room, how familiar.

The couch was near the door, here;
in front, a Turkish rug;
near the couch, two yellow vases on a shelf.
On the right, no, across from it, was an armoire with a mirror.
In the middle, the table where he wrote
and three wicker chairs.
Next to the window was the bed
where we made love so many times.

These sad things must still be somewhere.

Next to the window was the bed;
the afternoon sun spread across halfway.

. . . One afternoon at four o'clock, we separated,
just for a week. . . . Alas,
that week became forever.

[1919]

IMENOS

". . . We should love even more
pleasure attained morbidly, harmfully.
The body rarely feels what pleasure wants,
what morbidity and harm provide—
an erotic intensity that health does not know . . ."

Fragment from a letter
by young Imenos (among the patricians) notorious
in Syracuse for his depravity
in the depraved times of Michael the Third.

[1919]

OF THE JEWS (50 C.E.)

Painter and poet, runner and discus thrower,
beautiful as Endymion, Ianthis, son of Anthony,
was from a family friendly to the synagogue.

My most honest days
are when I leave behind the aesthetic search,
when I leave behind beautiful and hard Hellenism,
with its paramount focus
on perfectly made and mortal white limbs.
And I become the person I wish
always to remain—of the Jews, the holy Jews, the son.

His eager declaration: "Always
to remain of the Jews, the holy Jews—"

But he did not remain that way at all.
The Hedonism and Art of Alexandria
held him, a devoted son.

[1919]

TO STAY

The hour must have been one
or one-thirty at night.

                In a corner of the bar,
behind the wooden screen,
aside from the two of us, the place was completely empty,
and barely lit by a gas lamp.
The sleep-deprived waiter dozed in the doorway.

No one would see us. But also
we were so wild with desire
that we were unfit for caution.

Our clothes were half-open—we weren't wearing much
because divine July was fire hot.

Rapture of flesh between
half-open clothes,
a quick baring of skin—this ideal image
traverses twenty-six years; and now it comes
to stay in this poetry.

[1919]

121

OF DIMITRIOS SOTIR (162–150 B.C.E.)

All his hopes came out wrong!

He imagined his work renowned,
for he would end the humiliation that since the battle
of Magnesia oppressed his homeland.

Then Syria would be a powerful state again,
with its own armies, its own fleets,
large castles, and wealth.

He suffered, embittered in Rome.
In conversations with his friends,
the youth of great homes,
he saw through the subtlety and politeness
they showed him, the son
of King Selefkos Filopatros;
he understood there was always a secret
apathy toward the Hellenizing dynasties,
now declined, not destined for serious works,
wholly unfit to lead nations.
He withdrew, and alone—incensed—swore
it would not end up at all as they assumed;
look, he has the drive;
he will strive, act, exalt.

If only he finds a way to the East,
succeeds in escaping Italy,
all this power

in his soul, all this passion,
he will impart to his people.

Ah, if only he would find himself in Syria!
So young when he left his homeland,
he only vaguely remembered its face.
But in his mind he always pictured it
as something sacred, approached in awe,
a vision of the land of beauty, an image
of Greek cities and ports.

And now?
        Now despair and sorrow.
The young men in Rome were right.
It is impossible to sustain the dynasties
that arose from the Macedonian Conquest.

No matter. He tried,
struggled as much as he could.
And in his black disappointment
he reckons only one thing
with pride: even in failure
he shows the world the same indomitable courage.

The rest: dreams, labor in vain.
This Syria—it nearly seems not his homeland—
this is the country of Irakleides and Valas.

[1919]

ON THE SHIP

This small one certainly looks like him,
this portrait drawn in pencil.

Quickly done, on the ship's deck;
a magic afternoon.
All around us, the Ionian Sea.

It looks like him. Only I remember him more beautiful.
He was sensitive until suffering,
and this lighted his expression.
More beautiful he appears to me,
now when my soul recalls him, out of Time.

Out of Time. All these things are so old—
the sketch and the ship and the afternoon.

[1919]

IF TRULY DEAD

"Where has he withdrawn? Where did the Sage disappear?
After his countless miracles,
the fame of his teaching
broadcast in so many nations,
he suddenly hid and no one found out
with certainty what happened
(nor did anyone see his grave).
Some spread a rumor he died in Ephesus.
But Damis did not write it; Damis wrote nothing
about the death of Apollonios.
Others said he vanished in Lindos.
Or is that story
true that he ascended in Crete,
in the ancient temple of Diktynna.—
But still we have his miraculous,
his supernatural apparition
to a young student in Tyana.—
Perhaps the time has not come for him to return,
to show himself to the world again;
but perhaps transfigured
he circulates among us unrecognized.— But he will appear again
as he was, teaching the right path; and, of course, then
he will revive the worship of our gods,
and our refined Greek rituals."

So he dreamed in his shabby house—
after reading Philostratos's
On Apollonios of Tyana—

he, one of the few pagans,
one of the very few remaining. In any case—an insignificant
and timid man—to keep appearances,
he played the Christian and he, too, went to church.
It was the era when in utmost piety
old Justin was king,
and Alexandria, god-fearing city,
abhorred miserable idol worshippers.

[1920]

YOUNG MEN FROM SIDON (400 C.E.)

The actor they brought to entertain them
also recited some choice epigrams.

The hall opened onto the garden,
and a light fragrance of flowers
blended with the scent
of the five perfumed young men from Sidon.

The readings were from Meleagros, Krinagoras, and Rianos.
But when the actor recited,
"here lies Aeschylus, the Athenian, son of Euphorion"
(and perhaps stressed too much
"famous for his valor" and "sacred Marathonian grove"),
at once a lively young man, mad
for literature, leaped up and shouted:

"Oh, I don't like this quatrain.
Such expressions seem somewhat faint hearted.
I urge you to give your work all your strength,
all your care, and to recall your work again
in hardship or when your hour comes.
That's what I expect and demand of you.
Don't ever let the Shining
Word of Tragedy wholly leave your mind—
the Agamemnons, the admirable Prometheuses,
the performances of Orestes, Cassandra,

the *Seven against Thebes*—and keep in your memory
that in the ranks of soldiers and one of the masses,
you also fought against Datis and Artafernis."

[1920]

SO THEY WILL COME—

One candle is enough.   Its dim light
is more apt,   more genial
when Love comes,   when its Shadows come.

One candle is enough.   Tonight the room
should not have much light.   Fully inside the dream,
evocative,   in the low light—
inside the dream like this,   I will have visions
so Love will come,   so its Shadows will come.

[1920]

DAREIOS

The poet Fernazis composes
the crucial part of his epic poem:
how Dareios, son of Hystaspis,
took over the Persian Kingdom. (Our glorious King Mithridatis,
called Dionysos and Evpator, descends from that monarch.)
But here he needs philosophy, must analyze
the feelings Dareios would have had:
maybe arrogance and drunkenness; but no, rather
more like understanding the vanity of grandeur.
The poet thinks profoundly on the matter.

But he is interrupted. His servant runs in
and reports the portentous news:
war has broken out with the Romans.
Most of our army has crossed the border.

The poet is dumbfounded. What a catastrophe!
Now our glorious King
Mithridatis, called Dionysos and Evpator,
won't care about Greek poems.
During war—imagine, Greek poems.

Fernazis is fretful, impatient. Bad luck!
And just when it was certain his *Dareios*
would make his name and silence his malicious critics.
What a setback, a setback in his designs.

If it were only a setback, it wouldn't be so bad.
But who knows if we even have security
in Amisos. The city isn't well fortified.
The Romans are appalling enemies.
Can we Cappadocians contend with them?
Is it at all possible?
Is it possible for us to face their legions?
Great gods, protectors of Asia. Help us . . .

Yet despite all his distress and pessimism,
the poetic idea insistently comes and goes.
Of course, it was most probably arrogance and drunkenness.
That must be what Dareios felt, arrogance and drunkenness.

[1920]

ANNA KOMNINI

In the prologue to her *Alexiad*
Anna Komnini mourns her widowhood.

Her soul is vertigo. "And I have
rivers of tears," she says, "around
my eyes . . . alas, waves" of her life,
"alas, revolutions." Her grief burns her
"down to the marrow of the bone and the splitting" of her soul.

Yet the truth seems to be that this ambitious woman
knew only one intense sorrow;
that haughty Greek had only one deep regret
(even if she doesn't admit it)
that, with all her cleverness, she did not succeed
in gaining the crown. But the impudent John
snatched it from her very hands.

[1920]

A BYZANTINE NOBLEMAN IN EXILE
COMPOSING VERSES

Let the frivolous call me frivolous.
I have always been utterly meticulous about serious
matters. And I will insist,
no one knows the Church Fathers
or the Scriptures or the rules of the Synods better than I do.

Regarding each of his doubts,
each difficulty in church matters,
Votaniatis consulted me first, me first of all.
But in exile here (may the vicious Irini Doukas
burn in hell) and terribly bored,
it is not inappropriate that I would amuse myself
writing sextets and octets—
and I would amuse myself creating myths
about Hermes and Apollo and Dionysos
or about heroes of Thessaly and the Peloponnese;
and I would versify in strict iambs
in a manner—if you will permit me to say so—that the literati
of Constantinople lack the knowledge to compose.
This correctness, perhaps, is the reason they condemn me.

[1921]

THEIR BEGINNING

Their illicit pleasure was consummated.
They rose from the mattress
and quickly dressed without talking.
Separately, secretly, they leave the house; and as
they stride a bit anxiously in the street, it seems
as if they suspect something in them betrays
the kind of bed they lay in a short time ago.

Yet how the artist's life profits.
Tomorrow, the day after tomorrow, the strong lines
will be written whose beginning was here.

[1921]

THE FAVOR OF ALEXANDROS VALAS

Oh, I'm not upset a wheel
of my chariot broke, and I lost an absurd victory.
I'll spend the night with good wine,
among beautiful roses. Antioch is mine.
I'm the young man most glorified,
Valas's weakness, the one he adores.
Tomorrow, you'll see, they'll declare the race unfair.
(But if I were vulgar, if I secretly gave the order,
they'd have judged me the winner—the sycophants—
me and my lame chariot.)

[1921]

THE MELANCHOLY OF IASON KLEANDROS, POET IN KOMMAGINI, 595 C.E.

The aging of my body and my face
is a wound from a ghastly knife.
I have no perseverance at all.
I fall back on you, Art of Poetry,
who somehow knows drugs,
tries to put the pain to sleep through Fantasy and Word.

It's a wound from a ghastly knife.
Art of Poetry, bring me your drugs
that—for a short time—numb the wound.

[1921]

DIMARATOS

The subject, the Character of Dimaratos,
which Porfyry proposed in conversation,
was expressed in this way by the young sophist
(who afterward intended to develop it rhetorically):

"First he was a courtier of Dareios
and then of King Xerxes.
Now with Xerxes and his army—
see how at last Dimaratos will be vindicated.

A great injustice was committed against him.
He was Ariston's son. Shamelessly
his enemies bribed the oracle.
To deprive him of his kingship was not enough for them,
even when he finally succumbed and resolved
to live wearily as a private citizen,
they had to insult him in front of his people, too.
They had to humiliate him publicly at the festival.

So he serves Xerxes with much zeal.
He also will return to Sparta
with the great Persian army,
and be king as before. How he will oust him
immediately, how he will shame him,
that schemer Leotihidis!

So his days pass full of care;
how to give advice to the Persians, explain
how to conquer Greece.

Many worries, much thought, and this is why
the days of Dimaratos are so boring.
Many worries, much thought, and this is why
Dimaratos feels not even an instant of joy,
for joy is not what he feels.
(It isn't. Yet he won't acknowledge it.
How can he call it joy? at the culmination of his misery?)
When events show him clearly:
the Greeks will triumph."

[1921]

I BROUGHT TO ART

I sit and daydream.   Desires and sensations
I brought to Art—   some half-seen
faces or lines   of unfinished love,
some uncertain memories.   Let me give myself to Art.
Art knows how to give   Form to Beauty;
almost imperceptibly   completes life,
combining impressions,   combining the days.

[1921]

FROM THE SCHOOL OF THE CELEBRATED PHILOSOPHER

For two years he remained a student of Ammonios Sakkas,
but he got bored with philosophy and Sakkas.

Later he went into politics. But he gave it up.
The governor of the provinces was stupid;
the people around him, officious wooden statues
who merely looked serious,
who spoke thrice-barbarian Greek, the scum.

His curiosity was piqued
by the Church; to be baptized
and come off as a Christian. But soon
his opinion changed. He would surely quarrel
with his parents, who were ostentatious pagans,
and they would—awful thought—
cut off his extremely generous allowance.

But he should do something. He became a regular
of Alexandria's houses of corruption,
of every secret lair of debauchery.

His auspicious luck
endowed him with an extremely handsome figure.
And he enjoyed the divine gift.

His beauty would last
at least ten more years. Then—
he would return to Sakkas.

140

And if in the meantime the old man died,
he would go to another philosopher or sophist;
you always find someone to fit your purpose.

Or finally he might return
to politics—and admirably recall
his family traditions,
duty to country, and other such resounding notions.

[1921]

A CRAFTSMAN OF WINE BOWLS

On this wine bowl   made of pure silver
that was made   for the home of Irakleidis
where good taste   prevails supreme—
look, here are elegant flowers   and streams and thyme,
and in the center I have placed   a beautiful young man
naked, erotic;   he still dangles one of his calves
in the water.—   Oh, memory, I prayed
to find you my best   helper, so I might make
the face of the young man   I loved, as it was.
It turned out to be   a vast difficulty
because almost fifteen years   have passed since the day
he fell, a soldier   in the defeat of Magnesia.

[1921]

THOSE WHO FOUGHT FOR
THE ACHAIAN LEAGUE

You are brave, you who fought and fell in glory,
unafraid of those who triumphed everywhere.
You are blameless, if Diaios and Kritolaos are at fault.
When the Greeks want to boast, they will
declare: "Such are the men our nation breeds."
Praise for you will be this marvelous.—

Written by an Achaian in Alexandria,
the seventh year of the reign of Ptolemy Lathyros.

[1922]

TO ANTIOHOS EPIFANIS

The young Antiochian   said to the king,
"A dear hope   throbs in my heart,
Antiohos Epifanis.   The Macedonians,
the Macedonians   are back in the great struggle.
Let them win—   and I will give anyone who wants them,
the lion and the horses,   the coral Pan,
the elegant palace,   and the gardens of Tyre,
and everything else you've given me,   Antiohos Epifanis."

Perhaps the king   was somewhat moved.
But at once he remembered   his father and brother,
and didn't even answer.   Perhaps an eavesdropper
might recount something.—   At any rate, naturally,
at Pydna the horrible end   quickly came.

[1922]

IN AN OLD BOOK—

Forgotten between the pages of an old book—
nearly a hundred years old—
I found an unsigned watercolor.
A powerful artist must have painted the work,
entitled, *Presentation of Love*.

But a more fitting title is "love of the extreme sensualists."

Because it was obvious as you looked at the work
(you readily felt the artist's idea):
the adolescent in the painting
was not made for those who loved somewhat healthily,
staying within permissible boundaries—
with his deep brown eyes,
with the extraordinary beauty of his face,
the beauty of forbidden attractions,
with his ideal lips that give
pleasure to a loved body,
with his ideal limbs made for beds
that conventional morality calls shameless.

[1922]

IN DESPAIR

He's utterly lost him.   And now he seeks
his lips   in the lips
of each new lover.   In the union with each
new lover,   he seeks to fool himself
that he is the same young man,   the same one he gives himself to.

He's utterly lost him,   as if he never existed.
Because he wanted—he said—   he wanted to save himself
from the stigma   of that morbid pleasure,
from the stigma   of that shameful pleasure.
There was still time—   he said—to save himself.

He's utterly lost him,   as if he never existed.
In his fantasy,   in his hallucination,
he seeks his lips   in the lips of other young men;
he wants to feel   his passion again.

[1923]

146

FROM THE DRAWER

I was planning to hang it on a wall in my room.

But the dampness of the drawer damaged it.

I won't put this photograph in a frame.

I should have taken better care of it.

These lips, this face—
ah, if only the past would come back,
if only for a day, only for an hour.

I won't put this photograph in a frame.

I will suffer seeing it so marred.

Anyway, even if it were not damaged,
it would irk me to be cautious
in case some word, some tone of my voice betrayed me,
should someone ask about it.

[1923]

JULIAN SEEING INDIFFERENCE

"I see among us much indifference
toward the gods"—he says solemnly.
Indifference. But what did he expect, anyway?
Let him organize religion as much as he likes.
Let him write as much as he likes to the High Priest of Galatia
or other such figures, urging and directing them.
His friends were not Christians,
that was clear. But neither could they,
as he (who was brought up Christian),
play with a new church system,
absurd in both conception and practice.
They were Greeks, after all. Nothing in excess, Augustus.

[1923]

EPITAPH OF ANTIOHOS,
KING OF KOMMAGINI

After his mournful sister came back from the funeral
of the greatly learned King Antiohos of Kommagini,
a man who in life was temperate and mild,
she wanted an epitaph for him.
So the Ephesian sophist Kallistratos—
who often resided in the small state of Kommagini,
and whom the royal palace welcomed
time and again as a guest—
wrote it with the suggestions of the Syrian courtiers
and he sent it to the grand old lady.

"Let us aptly praise, O Kommaginians,
the glory of the beneficent King Antiohos.
He was a provident governor of the country.
He was just, wise, and brave.
He was also the best of all things, Greek.
Humanity possesses no quality more precious
and all beyond belongs to the gods."

[1923]

THEATER OF SIDON (400 C.E.)

The son of an honorable citizen—   above all, good-looking,
a youth in the theater,   pleasing in various ways—
sometimes I compose   fantastically daring lines
in the Greek language   that I circulate
extremely furtively—   gods! so that they won't be seen
by the gray-clad ones   jabbering of morals—
lines of pleasure,   the choice pleasure that produces
a barren love   and disapproval.

                                        [1923]

JULIAN IN NIKOMEDIA

Wrong and perilous matters:
the praises for Greek ideals;

the mysteries and the visits to the pagan temples;
the enthusiasm for the ancient gods;

the frequent conversations with Hrisanthios;
the theories of Maximus, a philosopher who's clever besides.

And here's the outcome. Gallos reveals his great
anxiety. Konstantios has some suspicions.

Oh, his advisors were not at all judicious.
This business—says Mardonis—is out of bounds.

And, for sure, the furor over it must stop.
Julian returns as a reader

to the church of Nikomedia
where in a great voice and with devotion

he intones many holy Scriptures
and the people marvel at his Christian piety.

[1924]

BEFORE TIME CHANGED THEM—

They were terribly sorry   when they parted.
It wasn't what they wanted   but circumstance.
The need to make a living   drove one of them
far away   to New York or Canada.
Of course, their love   was not the same as before.
Gradually, the attraction   cooled,
the attraction   cooled so much.
But to part—   they didn't want that.
It was circumstance.—   Or perhaps Chance
turned out to be an artist,   parting them now
before their feelings were snuffed out,   before Time changed them.
For each the other   will always stay
the twenty-four-year-old   beautiful boy.

[1924]

152

HE CAME TO READ

He came to read. Two or three books
are open: historians and poets.
But he'd hardly read ten minutes
when he stopped. He is half asleep
on the couch. He fully belongs to books—
but he is twenty-three years old, and very beautiful—
and this afternoon Eros came
to his ideal flesh, his lips.
Erotic heat came
to his flesh that is all beauty,
without ridiculous shame about the form of the pleasure.

[1924]

IN ALEXANDRIA, 31 B.C.E.

From his little village near the outskirts,
still dusty from the journey,

came the traveling salesman. And "Incense!" and "Gum!"
"Best Olive Oil!" and "Perfume for Hair!"

he cries out in the streets. But with the great hubbub
and the music and parades, how can he be heard?

The mob pushes him, drags him, hits him.
And when, totally dazed, he asks, "What is this madness?"

someone hurls at him the gigantic lie
from the palace—Antony triumphed in Greece.

[1924]

IOANNIS KANTAKOUZINOS TRIUMPHS

He looks at the fields he still owns—
the wheat, the animals, the fruit-laden trees;
and farther away, his ancestral home,
full of clothing, precious furniture, and silver vessels.

They'll take it all away—Jesus Christ!—now they'll take it all away.

Perhaps Kantakouzinos would pity him,
if he threw himself at his feet. They say he's merciful,
very merciful. But what about those around him? And the army?
Or should he prostrate himself and plead before Lady Irini?

Idiot! to be drawn into Anna's party—
If only Lord Andronikos had never married her.
Have we seen progress from her actions? Or humanity?
Not even the Franks have any respect for her.
Her ridiculous plans, all her preparations absurd.
While they threatened the world from Constantinople,
Kantakouzinos crushed them, Lord Ioannis crushed them.

And to think he had in mind to side with Lord Ioannis!
He would have done it, and now he'd be happy,
ever a great lord and secure,
if at the last moment the bishop hadn't swayed him
with his imposing authority
and his information wrong from beginning to end
and his promises and his nonsense.

[1924]

155

TEMETHOS, ANTIOCHIAN, 400 C.E.

Verses of young Temethos,   lovestruck.
With the title "Emonidis"—   the adored lover
of Antiohos Epifanis,   a gorgeous
young man from Samosata.   But if the lines come out
ardent, emotional   it is because Emonidis
(from that ancient   epoch,
the one-hundred-thirty-seventh   year of the Greek reign!—
maybe a bit before)   was put in the poem
merely as a name,   a very apt one, nonetheless.
The poem expresses   the love of Temethos,
his beautiful and worthy love.   We the initiated,
his close friends,   we the initiated
know for whom   the lines were written.
The unsuspecting Antiochians   read "Emonidis."

[1925]

156

OF COLORED GLASS

I am so moved by a detail
in the coronation at Vlachernai of Ioannis Kantakouzinos
and Irini, daughter of Andronikos Asan.
As they had very few precious stones
(poverty was great in our suffering state)
they wore artificial gems. Abundant pieces of glass:
red, green, or light blue. There is nothing
degrading or undignified,
as I see it, about these small pieces
of colored glass. On the contrary they seem
like a sad protest
against the unjust fate of the crowned.
They are symbols of what was fitting for them to have,
what was absolutely right for them to have
for their coronation, a Lord Ioannis Kantakouzinos
and a Lady Irini, daughter of Andronikos Asan.

[1925]

THE TWENTY-FIFTH YEAR OF HIS LIFE

He goes to the taverna regularly
where they met last month.
He asked about him, but they had nothing to tell him.
From their words, he understood he'd met
a completely unknown person,
one of the many unknown and suspect
youthful faces that passed through there.
Yet he goes to the taverna regularly, at night,
and sits and watches the doorway;
he watches the doorway until he's weary.
Maybe he'll come in. Tonight maybe he'll come.

For close to three weeks he does this.
His mind is sick with lust.
The kisses stay on his lips.
All his flesh suffers from relentless desire.
The touch of that body is all over him.
He wants to merge with him again.

He tries, of course, not to give himself away,
but sometimes he almost doesn't care.
Besides, he knows the hazard he risks,
and has resigned himself to it. It's not unlikely
his kind of life will bring him ruinous scandal.

[1925]

ON AN ITALIAN SHORE

Kimos, son of Menedoros,   a young Greek-Italian
spends his life   amusing himself,
as is customary   for such young men
from Greater Greece   brought up in lavish wealth.

But today,   despite his nature,
he is gloomy and downcast.   Near the shore,
in acute melancholy,   he sees them unload
the ships bearing the spoils   of the Peloponnese.

Plunder from Greece;   the spoils of Corinth.

Ah, today, of course,   it is not right,
it is not possible   for the young Greek-Italian
to have any desire   to amuse himself.

[1925]

IN THE BORING VILLAGE

In the boring village where he works,
a clerk in a general store—
so young, and he is waiting
for two or three months to pass,
another two or three months, until business slackens,
until he can set off for the city and thrust himself
right into the action and entertainment.
In the boring village where he is waiting—
tonight he's fallen into bed, full of erotic desire
all his youth keen with desire for the flesh,
all his beautiful youth in beautiful intensity.
Pleasure has come in his sleep; in his sleep
he sees and possesses the face, the flesh he wants.

[1925]

APOLLONIOS OF TYANA IN RHODES

Apollonios was speaking
about proper education and training
to a young man building a luxurious
house in Rhodes. "As for me,"
the Tyanian finally said, "when I'm in a temple,
it's more pleasurable to see a statue,
however small, made of gold and ivory,
than a large one made of clay that is vulgar."

Made of "clay" and the "vulgar"—disgusting—
yet a good many (who lack enough training)
are deceived by the sham. Made of clay and vulgar.

[1925]

THE ILLNESS OF KLEITOS

Kleitos—an amiable young man,
about twenty-three years old,
with an excellent upbringing, with a rare knowledge of Greek—
is critically ill. The fever struck him
that mowed down Alexandria this year.

The fever struck him when he was morally exhausted, as well,
for he sorrowed that his companion, a young actor,
no longer loved him and wanted him.

He is critically ill. His parents tremble for their son.

And an old servant who raised him
also trembles for the life of Kleitos.
In her terrible anxiety
an idol comes to mind
whom she worshipped as a little girl,
before coming here to be a servant
in the house of distinguished Christians, before she converted.
Secretly, she takes some cake and wine and honey.
She places them before the idol. Whatever parts of the prayer
she remembers, she chants: beginnings, ends. The fool
does not comprehend the black demon does not care
whether or not a Christian is cured.

[1926]

IN A TOWNSHIP IN ASIA MINOR

The news of the naval battle in Actium
was certainly unexpected.
But there is no need for us to compose a new document.
Only the name should be changed. Instead, there
in the last lines, "Having liberated the Romans
from ruinous Octavian,
that parody of Caesar,"
we will now insert "Having liberated the Romans
from ruinous Antony."
The whole text fits together beautifully

"To the victor, most glorious,
unsurpassable in every military venture,
marvelous in great political actions,
on whose behalf the township fervently wished
Antony would prevail."
Here, as we said, is the change: "To Caesar,
regarded as the paramount gift from Zeus,
to the powerful protector of the Greeks,
who looks on our Greek customs favorably,
beloved in every Greek land,
the one most worthy of high praise
and of lengthy histories of his deeds,
in Greek, in both verse and in prose,
in Greek, the vehicle of fame,"
etcetera, etcetera. Everything fits together brilliantly.

[1926]

163

THE PRIEST OF SERAPEION

My old and good father
who always loved me the same way—
I mourn my old and good father
who died two days ago, a little before daybreak.

Jesus Christ, my daily task is to keep
the commandments of your holiest church
in my every act, every word,
every thought. And those who deny you
I loathe—but now I mourn,
I wail for my father, Christ,
although he was—dreadful to say—
a priest in the accursed Serapeion.

[1926]

IN THE BARS

I wallow in the bars   and brothels
of Beirut.   I didn't want to live
in Alexandria.   Tamidis left me
and went off with the Prefect's son,   so he'll get
a villa on the Nile,   a mansion in the city.
It wouldn't do to stay   in Alexandria.
I wallow in the bars   and brothels
of Beirut.   In cheap debauchery
I live a low life.   The only thing that saves me—
like lasting beauty,   like lingering perfume
on my flesh—   is that Tamidis was mine
for two years,   the most superb youth,
mine, and not for a house   or a villa on the Nile.

[1926]

A GRAND PROCESSION OF
PRIESTS AND LAYMEN

A procession of priests and laymen,
with all professions represented,
passes through the streets, squares, and gates
of the renowned city of Antioch.
At the beginning of the imposing grand procession
a beautiful white-clad adolescent boy
holds up the Cross,
our strength and our hope, the Holy Cross.
The pagans, who were arrogant until now,
slyly, timidly, hastily
move away from the procession.
Away from us, let them always stay away from us
(for as long as they don't renounce their error).
The Holy Cross advances—and brings solace and joy
in every quarter where Christians live in godliness:
the devout come from the doors of their homes
and, full of exultation, bow before it—
the strength, the salvation of the world, the Cross.

It is an annual Christian festival.
But look, today, it is celebrated more conspicuously.
At last the state is liberated.
The vile, the abominable
Julian is no longer king.

Let us pray for most pious Jovian.

[1926]

A SOPHIST LEAVING SYRIA

Esteemed sophist,   now you are leaving Syria
and plan to write   about Antioch,
it is worthwhile to refer   to Mevis in your work.
The renowned Mevis   who doubtless is
the most beautiful   and beloved young man
in all Antioch.   No other boy
who leads that kind of life,   no one is paid
as richly as he.   To have Mevis
for only two, three days,   very often they give him
up to one hundred staters.—   I said, in Antioch,
but in Alexandria as well,   but beyond that even in Rome,
you won't find a young man   as desired as Mevis.

[1926]

JULIAN AND THE ANTIOCHIANS

The "Chi" they say did not harm the city, nor did the "Kappa" . . . but
finding interpreters . . . we were taught that the letters are the initial
letters of names: the first denotes Christ and the second Konstantios.
                                   —Julian, *Misopogon, or the Beard-Hater*

Could they ever denounce
their beautiful lifestyle?
The variety of their daily amusements? Their brilliant
theater that fused Art with their erotic appetites!

They were immoral up to a point—perhaps they exceeded
that point—but they had the satisfaction that their life
was the notorious life of Antioch,
the sensual, the perfectly tasteful.

To deny all this in order to devote themselves to what?

His empty words about false gods,
his boring grandstanding,
his childish fear of the theater,
his graceless prudishness, his ridiculous beard.

Oh, of course, they preferred the "Chi,"
Oh, of course, they preferred the "Kappa" a hundred times more.

                                   [1926]

168

ANNA DALASSINI

On the gold seal Alexios Komninos issued
to gloriously honor his mother—
the most intelligent Lady Anna Dalassini,
distinguished in her works and her ethics—
there are many accolades.
Here let us select one
beautiful and noble phrase:
"Those cold words, 'mine' or 'yours,'
were never pronounced between us."

[1927]

DAYS OF 1896

He was utterly disgraced.   His erotic inclinations,
sternly forbidden   and held in contempt,
(but nonetheless innate)   were the cause:
society was   extremely prudish.
Gradually, he lost   the little money he had,
then his rank,   then his reputation.
He was almost thirty   and had not worked
even a year,   at least not at a legitimate job.
Sometimes he earned   his expenses
for mediations   considered shameful.
He was reduced to the type   who most likely would
thoroughly discredit you   if you were seen with him too often.

But this isn't all of it.   It's not right.
The memory of his beauty   is worth more.
There's another slant   and if seen from that perspective
he appears likeable;   he appears simple and pure,
a child of love   who with no forethought
put his pure flesh   his pure pleasure
above his honor,   and his reputation.
And his reputation?   But society,
completely priggish,   came to stupid conclusions.

[1927]

TWO YOUNG MEN, TWENTY-THREE TO TWENTY-FOUR YEARS OLD

At ten-thirty he was at the café
and he waited for him to appear before long.
Midnight passed—and still he waited for him.
One-thirty passed and the café
was almost completely empty.
He was tired of reading newspapers
mechanically. Of his miserable three shillings,
he had only one left: he waited so long he spent
the rest of his money on coffees and cognacs.
He smoked all his cigarettes.
All that waiting exhausted him. Because
alone for hours, as he was, he started
to be overwhelmed by disturbing thoughts
of his outcast life.

But when he saw his friend come in—instantly
the weariness, the boredom, the thoughts vanished.

His friend brought unhoped-for news.
He'd won sixty pounds playing cards.

Their beautiful faces, their exquisite youth,
the artful love they shared
were refreshed, revived, uplifted
by the sixty pounds won at the gambling house.

And full of joy and power, feeling and beauty
they went—not to the houses of their honest families

(where, anyway, they were no longer welcome):
they went to a very particular house of vice
they knew of and asked for a room
and expensive drinks, and they drank again.

And when the expensive drinks were gone
and when the hour approached four,
they gave themselves blissfully to love.

[1927]

GREEK SINCE ANCIENT TIMES

Antioch boasts   superb buildings,
beautiful roads,   the surrounding
marvelous countryside,   and the great multitude
who lives there.   It boasts it is the seat
of glorious kings,   artists,
and sages   and enormously wealthy
and astute merchants.   But immeasurably
above all, Antioch   boasts it is a city
Greek since ancient times,   a relative of Argos
through Ione,   which was founded by Argive colonists
in honor   of Inahos's daughter.

[1927]

DAYS OF 1901

What was extraordinary about him was that—
despite all his dissolution,
his great sexual experience,
the habitual harmony
between his age and his attitude—
there were times—though very rare,
of course—when he gave the impression
his flesh was almost untouched.

His twenty-nine-year-old beauty
so tried by pleasure
at times reminded you
of an adolescent who for the first time—
somewhat awkwardly—delivers his pure body to love.

[1927]

YOU DID NOT KNOW

About our religious beliefs—
the hollow Julian said, "I read, I knew,
I dissented." As if he annihilated us
with his "dissent," that ridiculous man.

Yet such wisecracks had no resonance for us
Christians. We instantly retorted, "You read, but you did not know,
because if you knew, you would not dissent."

[1928]

A YOUNG MAN, AN ARTIST OF THE WORD, IN HIS TWENTY-FIFTH YEAR

Mind, work as best you can.—
Spent by half pleasure,
he's in a maddening position.
He kisses the beloved face every day,
his hands touch the most exquisite limbs.
He's never loved with such great
passion, but misses love's beautiful
fulfillment, misses the fulfillment
both of them should intensely desire.

(They aren't equally given to deviant pleasure.
Only he is utterly overcome.)

So he's spent, tense
and, what's more, out of work, to make it worse.
He borrows some small amounts
of money with difficulty (he almost
begs) and barely scrapes by.
He kisses the adored lips. He finds
pleasure—though he feels now
the other merely consents—on the exquisite body.
And then he drinks and smokes, drinks and smokes,
drags himself to the cafés all day long,
drags himself around, tedium fading his beauty.—
Mind, work as best you can.

[1928]

IN SPARTA

King Kleomenis didn't know—didn't dare—
didn't know how to utter such a word
to his mother: the Ptolemy demanded
that she be sent to Egypt and be held hostage
to guarantee their treaty,
a very humiliating, unbefitting thing.
And he was always about to talk and always faltering
and starting to say and always stopping.

But the superb woman understood him
(she had also heard some pertinent rumors),
and encouraged him to explain himself.
And she laughed and said, of course, she'd go
and moreover she was glad that in her old age
she could still be useful to Sparta.

As for humiliation—well, she was indifferent to it.
A king of the new Lagidis dynasty was certainly incapable
of comprehending the Spartan ethos.
So his demand could not
in fact humiliate a Preeminent Great Lady
like her, the mother of a Spartan king.

[1928]

PORTRAIT OF A TWENTY-THREE-YEAR-OLD MAN, PAINTED BY HIS FRIEND THE SAME AGE, AN AMATEUR

He finished the portrait   yesterday at noon.
Now he looks at it in detail.   He made him in a gray
suit, unbuttoned—   deep gray—with no
waistcoat and tie.   In a rose-colored
shirt, open   so that something of the beauty
of his chest and neck   is revealed.
The right side of his forehead   is almost entirely
covered by his hair,   his beautiful hair
(parted the way   he likes it this year).
The portrait captures   the fully hedonistic feel
he wanted to put in   when he did the eyes,
when he did the lips . . .   his mouth, his lips
made for fulfilling   rare eroticism.

[1928]

IN A LARGE GREEK COLONY, 200 B.C.E.

There is not the slightest doubt
that things in the Colony don't go as one would wish,
and though we move forward, anyway,
perhaps, as not a few think, the time has come
for us to bring in a Political Reformer.

Yet the obstacle and difficulty
is that they make a big deal
out of everything, these Reformers.
(It would be a stroke of good luck
if one never needed them.) Everything,
every little thing, they ask about and examine,
and instantly radical reforms come to mind
and they demand they be implemented without delay.

They lean toward sacrifice.
Give up that property of yours,
your owning it is risky:
such possessions are harmful to the Colonies.
Give up that income
and that coming from it,
and this third one, as a natural consequence.
They are essential, but it can't be helped;
they create an adverse liability for you.

And as they proceed in their inspection,
they find (then find again) needless things,
which they demand must go—
things that nevertheless are hard to dismiss.

And when, with good luck, they finish their work,
having ordered and pared everything down to the last detail,
they leave, taking away their rightful wages, as well.
We'll see what remains, after
so much expert surgery.

Perhaps the time has not yet come.
Let's not rush; haste is a dangerous thing.
Premature measures bring regret.
Certainly and unfortunately, there is much disorder in the Colony.
But is there anything human without imperfection?
And, anyway, look, we're moving forward.

[1928]

A PRINCE FROM WESTERN LIBYA

He was generally liked in Alexandria
the ten days he stayed there—
Aristomenis, the son of Menelaos.
Like his name, his attire was fittingly Greek.
He gladly accepted honors, but
he did not seek them. He was modest.
He bought Greek books,
especially history and philosophy.
Above all, he was a man of few words.
He must be deep in thought, it was rumored,
and for such people it was natural not to talk a lot.

He was neither deep in thought, nor anything else.
An ordinary, ridiculous man,
he assumed a Greek name, dressed like the Greeks,
he more or less learned to comport himself like the Greeks;
and his soul trembled that by chance
he would ruin the fairly good impression he had made
by speaking Greek with terrible barbarisms,
and the Alexandrians would make fun of him,
as is usual with them, those frightful people.

That is why he limited himself to few words,
attending anxiously to conjunctions and pronunciation;
and he was more than a little bored,
the talk heaped up inside him.

[1928]

KIMON, SON OF LEARHOS, TWENTY-TWO, STUDENT OF GREEK LETTERS (IN KYRINI)

"My end came   when I was happy.
Ermotelis took me   as his inseparable friend.
My very last days   despite his pretending
he was not worried   I often noticed
his eyes red from crying.   When he thought
I was dozing off   he threw himself like a madman
on the edge of my bed.   But we were both
young, the same age,   twenty-three years old.
Fate is the traitor.   Perhaps another passion
would have taken   Ermotelis away from me.
My end was good;   I was in indivisible love."

This is the epitaph   of Marilos Aristodimos,
who died   a month ago in Alexandria
and that I, Kimon, his cousin,   received in my grief.
The writer, a poet I know,   sent it to me.
He sent it to me   because he knew
I was a relative of Marilos;   he didn't know anything else.
My soul is full   of sorrow for Marilos.
We grew up   together like brothers.
I am deeply melancholy.   His premature death
erased   all my resentments . . .
all my resentments   toward Marilos—although
he stole away Ermotelis's   love for me,
so that now even if Ermotelis   wants me again
it won't be the same at all.   I know
my sensitive character.   The image of Marilos
will come between us,   and I'll think

he's saying to me,   Look, are you satisfied now.
Look, you've taken him back   as you wanted, Kimon.
Look, you no longer   have cause to denigrate me.

[1928]

ON THE MARCH TO SINOPI

Mithridatis, glorious and powerful,
master of great cities,
commander of strong armies and fleets,
on his way to Sinopi, goes on very remote
country roads
where a seer has his home.

Mithridatis sends one of his officers
to ask the seer how many more possessions
he will acquire, how many more forces.

He sent his officer, and then
he continued on his march to Sinopi.

The seer retired to a secret room.
After about a half an hour he came out
concerned, and said to the officer,
"I have not been able to see clearly enough to be satisfied.
Today is not the right day.
I saw some shadowy things. I didn't understand well.
But I believe, let the king be content with all he has.
More will put him in danger.
Remember to tell him this, officer:
with all he has, for God's sake, let him be content!
Fortune suddenly changes.
Tell King Mithridatis:

very rarely is one like his ancestor's noble friend found,
who just in time uses his lance to write
salvation in the dust, *Flee, Mithridatis.*"

[1928]

DAYS OF 1909, '10, AND '11

He was the son of an oppressed, wretchedly poor sailor
(from an island in the Aegean).
He worked in a blacksmith's shop. He wore rags.
His work shoes were torn and pitiful,
his hands stained with rust and oil.

In the evening, after he closed the shop,
if there was something he particularly wanted,
some tie, a somewhat expensive one,
some tie for Sunday,
if he saw some beautiful blue shirt
in a shop window and yearned for it,
he sold his body for one or two crowns.

I ask myself if in ancient times
glorious Alexandria had young men more sublime,
a more perfect boy than him, who went to waste:
clearly, there is no statue or painting of him;
thrown into a blacksmith's shabby shop,
with the back-breaking work,
the vulgar orgies, the hardship, he was quickly spent.

[1928]

MYRIS: ALEXANDRIA, 340 C.E.

When I heard the disaster that Myris was dead,
I went to his house, though I avoid
entering Christian houses,
especially when they mourn or celebrate.

I stood in the hall. I didn't want
to go farther inside because I noticed
the relatives of the deceased looking at me
with obvious bewilderment and displeasure.

They had laid him out in a large room
(I could see a bit
from where I stood) full of precious rugs
and vessels made of silver and gold.

I stood and cried in a corner of the hall.
And I thought without Myris
our get-togethers and outings
would no longer be worth anything;
and I thought I'd no longer see him
at our beautiful and lascivious all-night parties,
nor happy, nor laughing, nor reciting verses
with his perfect feel for Greek meter;
and I thought I lost his beauty
forever, I lost forever
the young man I passionately adored.

Some old women near me were talking in low voices
about the last day he lived—
Christ's name was always on his lips;
in his hand he held a cross.
Then four Christian priests
entered the room, ardently saying prayers
and entreating Jesus
or Mary (I don't know their religion well).

Of course, we knew Myris was a Christian.
We knew from the first moment
he joined our group, the year before last.
But he behaved just as we did.
He was the most dissolute of all of us in his pleasures,
lavishly throwing away his money on entertainment.
He was careless about the world's regard;
he threw himself willingly into nighttime street brawls
when it happened that our gang
met a rival one.
He never spoke of his religion.
In fact, one day we told him
we would take him with us to the Serapeion.
But he seemed annoyed
with our joke. I remember now.
Ah, and another two incidents come to mind.
When we made libations to Poseidon,
he withdrew from our circle and looked away.
When one of us said fervently

may our group be
favored and protected by the great
and most beautiful Apollo—Myris whispered
(the others didn't hear), "Except me."

In resounding voices the Christian priests
prayed for the soul of the young man.—
I noticed with how much diligence
and intense concern for the rites
of their religion they prepared
everything for a Christian burial.
And suddenly a strange sensation
took hold of me. Vaguely, I felt
as if Myris were leaving me;
I felt as if he, as a Christian, were joining
his own, and I were becoming
a stranger, a total stranger. I also felt
a doubt seize me: perhaps I was deluded
by my passion, and I was always a stranger to him.—
I flung myself out of their awful house;
I left quickly before the memory of Myris
was snatched away, before their Christianity falsified it.

[1929]

ALEXANDROS IANNAIOS
AND ALEXANDRA

Successful and fully satisfied,
King Alexandros Iannaios
and his wife Queen Alexandra
passed through the streets of Jerusalem,
passed through preceded by music
and all kinds of grandeur and luxury.
The work begun by the great Judas Maccabeus
and his four renowned brothers,
and later unyieldingly carried on in the midst
of many dangers and many difficulties,
succeeded splendidly.
Now nothing unseemly remains.
All submission to the arrogant
monarch of Antioch is over. Look,
King Alexandros Iannaios
and his wife Queen Alexandra,
in every way equal to the Seleucids.
Good Jews, pure Jews, above all, faithful Jews.
But as circumstances demand,
proficient in the Greek language
and associating with the Greek and Hellenizing
monarchs—but as equals, let it be known.
Truly, it succeeded splendidly,
it succeeded most brilliantly,
the work begun by the great Judas Maccabeus
and his four renowned brothers.

[1929]

190

BEAUTIFUL WHITE FLOWERS BECAME HIM

He went to the café   where they used to go together—
where three months ago   his friend said to him,
"We don't have a penny.   We're two very poor
kids, lowered   to the cheap clubs.
I'm telling you in all honesty,   I can't go
around with you. I'm letting you   know another wants me."
The other had promised him   two suits and some
silk handkerchiefs.—   He moved heaven and earth
to win him back again,   and found twenty pounds;
he came back to him   for the twenty pounds
but also,   for the old friendship,
the old love,   the deep feelings.
The "other" was a liar,   a real bum;
he had only one suit   made for him, and
even that under pressure   and with a thousand pleas.

But right now he doesn't   want the suit at all,
and he doesn't want   the silk handkerchiefs at all,
and not the twenty pounds at all,   and not even twenty piastres.

Sunday they buried him   at ten in the morning.
Sunday they buried him   almost a week ago.

On his cheap coffin   he laid flowers,
beautiful white flowers   that so became
his beauty   and his twenty-two years.

When he went in the evening   he had business,
a need to earn his bread—   in the café
where they used to go together: a knife in his heart,
the black café   where they used to go together.

COME, O KING OF THE LACEDAIMONIANS

Kratisiklia did not deign
for the people to see her crying and mourning,
and she walked magnificent and silent.
Nothing of her sorrow and torment
showed on her serene face.
Nevertheless for one moment she did not bear up;
and before she boarded the vile ship to go to Alexandria,
she took her son to the temple of Poseidon
and when they were alone, she embraced him
and kissed him, "in great pain," said
Plutarch, "and deeply afflicted."
Yet her strong character persevered
and taking hold of herself the marvelous woman
said to Kleomenis, "Come, O King
of the Lacedaimonians, so when we go out
no one will see us in tears
nor doing anything unworthy of Sparta.
For this is between us alone;
on the other hand, fate will be as God gives it."

And she boarded the ship headed toward "the given."

[1929]

193

IN THE SAME SPACE

Surroundings of the house, meeting places, neighborhoods
that I see and where I walk, for years and years.

I created you with joys and sorrows,
so many events, so many things.

And you've made yourself all feeling for me.

[1929]

THE MIRROR IN THE FRONT HALL

In the front hall of the opulent house
was an immense mirror, very old,
purchased at least eighty years ago.

A gorgeous boy, a tailor's employee
(on Sundays, an amateur athlete)
stood holding a parcel. He delivered
it to one of the household, who carried it
inside to get a receipt. The tailor's employee
stayed alone and waited.
He drew near the mirror and looked at himself
and straightened his tie. After five minutes
someone brought the receipt. He took it and left.

The old mirror had seen and seen
thousands of things and faces
in its many years of existence—
and nevertheless the old mirror rejoiced now,
proud to have held the reflection
of absolute beauty for a few minutes.

[1930]

HE ASKED ABOUT THE QUALITY—

He came out of the office where he was employed
in an unimportant and poorly paid position
(up to eight pounds a month, with tips);
when he finished his tedious work
that kept him stooped all afternoon,
he came out at seven, and sauntered slowly,
gazing idly in the street. Beautiful
and interesting, he carried himself
as if he'd reached his full sensual potential.
He turned twenty-nine a month ago.

He gazed idly in the street, and down the poor alleys
that led to his rooms.

Passing by a small shop
where they sold cheap
and inferior goods for laborers,
he saw a face inside, he saw a shape
that moved him to enter, and he acted as if
he wanted to see colored handkerchiefs.

He asked about the quality of the handkerchiefs
and what they cost
in a choked voice
almost erased by desire.
And the answers came the same way,
absently, in a lowered voice,
with an implied consent.

They kept talking about the merchandise—but
their sole aim: to touch hands
on top of the handkerchiefs, to draw
their faces together, their lips, as if by accident;
a fleeting touch of their limbs.

Quickly and furtively so the shopkeeper
sitting in the back would not notice.

[1930]

THEY SHOULD HAVE CARED

I've fallen so low, I'm poor and almost homeless.
This fatal city, Antioch,
ate up all my money:
this fatal place with its expensive life.

But I'm young and in excellent health.
I speak wonderful Greek
(I know—truly know—Aristotle, Plato,
the orators, the poets, whomever you may name).
I have an idea of military arts
and I'm friends with mercenary leaders.
I'm in-the-know in administration.
Last year I spent six months in Alexandria;
I know something of its affairs (and this is useful):
the ambitions of Kakergetis, his dirty deals, and so on.

So I deem myself fully capable
and right to serve my country,
the homeland I love, Syria.

Whatever task they give me, I will try
to be useful to my country. That's my intent.
But if they thwart me with their schemes—
and we know them, those fine friends.—
(Do you want to talk about it now?)
If they thwart me, is it my fault?

First, I'll approach Zabinas,
and if that fool doesn't appreciate me,
I'll go to his rival, Grypos.
And if that idiot doesn't appoint me,
I'll go straight to Hyrkanos.

In any case, one of the three will want me.

And my conscience is clear
for treating my choice lightly.
All three harm Syria equally.

But is it my fault I'm a ruined man?
If I'm down on my luck and strive to fix my life?
The all-powerful gods should have cared
to have created a fourth good person.
I would have gladly gone to him.

[1930]

ACCORDING TO THE RECIPES OF THE ANCIENT GRECO-SYRIAN MAGICIANS

"What essence of magic herbs
can be found," asked the aesthete,
"what essence made according to the recipes
of the ancient Greco-Syrian magicians
might bring me back again to my twenty-third year
for a day (if its power won't last longer)
or even for an hour,
might bring my twenty-two-year-old friend
back to me again, his beauty, his love?

What essence made according to the recipes
of the ancient Greco-Syrian magicians can be found
that in keeping with the return to the past
will bring back our small room?"

[1931]

IN 200 B.C.E.

"Alexander, son of Philip and the Greeks, except the Lacedaimonians—"

We can very well imagine
that in Sparta they were wholly indifferent
to this inscription. "Except the Lacedaimonians"—
but naturally. The Spartans would not be
led and ordered about
like valuable servants. At any rate,
without a Spartan king as leader,
a Panhellenic campaign
would not seem of great consequence to them.

Ah, of course, "except the Lacedaimonians."

This, too, is a stance. It's understood.

This way, "except the Lacedaimonians" at Granikos,
then later at Issus, then the final battle
when the formidable army
that the Persians rallied at Arbela was swept away,
the army that from Arbela set out for victory was swept away.

And from that marvelous Panhellenic campaign—
victorious, most brilliant,
most renowned, glorified,
as no one before was glorified,
incomparable—we were born,
the great new Hellenic world.

We, the Alexandrians, the Antiochians,
the Seleucids, and the numerous
other Greeks in Egypt and Syria
and in Media and in Persia, and so many more.
With our far-flung lands,
with the flexible action of judicious adjustments.
And we carried the Common Greek Language
as far as Bactria, as far as the Indians.

Should we speak of the Lacedaimonians now!

[1931]

DAYS OF 1908

That year he found himself without work;
so he lived by playing cards,
backgammon, and borrowing money.

He was offered a position, three pounds a month,
in a small stationery store.
But he turned it down without hesitating.
It was not fitting. That was no salary for him,
a young man with enough education, and twenty-five years old.

He won—or didn't win—two or three shillings a day.
From cards and backgammon, what could the kid earn
in the working-class cafés of his social level,
however cleverly he played, however stupid the players he chose.
His borrowing money is not worth mentioning.
He rarely came up with a five-pound note, more often, half that
and sometimes he settled for just a shilling.

For a week, sometimes longer,
he escaped from the horrible late nights,
and he cooled off in the sea, swimming in the morning.

His clothes were in an awful state.
He always wore the same suit, a very faded
cinnamon-colored suit.

Ah, summer days of 1908,
what good taste to remove
the cinnamon-colored suit from your sight.

Your sight kept him as he was
when he threw off
the unworthy clothes and mended underwear.
And he remains all naked, faultlessly beautiful, a marvel.
His hair uncombed, standing up a bit,
his limbs a little tanned from the sun,
from being naked in the morning sea, from swimming at the beach.

[1932]

IN THE SUBURBS OF ANTIOCH

We were surprised in Antioch when we learned
of Julian's latest antics.

At Dafni Apollo made himself clear to Julian.
He didn't want to pronounce the oracle (who cares!),
he didn't intend to prophesy, if his temple
in Dafni weren't purified first.
He said the neighboring dead annoyed him.

In Dafni there are many tombs.—
One of the dead
was the marvelous glory of our church,
the saint, the triumphant martyr Vavylas.

The false god alluded to him, the one he feared.
As long as he felt him near, he didn't dare
speak his prophesies, not a word.
(The false gods tremble before our martyrs.)

The godless Julian rolled up his sleeves,
a nervous wreck, and shouted, "Hoist him up, take him away,
dig up this Vavylas immediately.
Listen here. Apollo is annoyed.
Hoist him up, seize him now,
unearth him, take him wherever you want.
Dig him up, throw him out. Are we playing now?
Apollo said to purify the temple."

We took it away, carried the saintly relic elsewhere.
We took it away, carried it in love and honor.

And really the temple thrived beautifully.
It wasn't long before a huge fire
broke out, a terrible fire:
and both Apollo and the temple burned up.

The idol was ashes, to sweep into the garbage.

Julian burst with rage and he spread the word—
what else could he do—that we, the Christians,
set the fire. Let him talk.
It's unproven. Let him talk.
What's vital is he burst with rage.

[1935]

A NOTE ON THE
TRANSLITERATION OF NAMES

The transliteration of Greek names into Roman letters is in flux, just as is language itself. As a quick survey of recent translations from the Greek will reveal, there are no fast rules and little consistency. Because Cavafy is a Modern Greek poet, who used the demotic and whose subject matter so frequently concerns Hellenization, I have wherever possible used the Greek rather than the Latin spellings. For example, I transliterate Kleopatra (Cleopatra), with a K rather than a C, because the change in the first letter does not render the name unrecognizable. With very familiar proper names, such as Julian (Ioulianos) or Constantine the Great (Megas Konstantinos), Athens (Athena) or Rhodes (Rhodos), whose Latinized names have entered the English language, I have kept the traditional spellings, in order to avoid confusing or jarring the reader. The question of how to transliterate the names of dynasties, such as the Ptolemaic or the Seleucid (Selefkid), is particularly vexing, as the Latinized spellings are still most often used in historical texts. I have used the Latin names in reference to dynasties (as in "The Glory of the Ptolemies"), but when it comes to individual names, I have chosen to use the Greek ("I am Lagidis, king," in the same poem, as opposed to "Lagus"). The subject of "The Glory of the Ptolemies" is which dynasty, the Ptolemaic or the Seleucid, is more Hellenized, so to Latinize these Greek names seems to move directly against the tone and poetics of the work. So that a reader who wishes to engage in further study will have all the pertinent information, the notes provide the Greek spellings in parentheses, when I have used the more familiar names (as in Julian and Constantine above); when I have used Greek spellings, as in Theokritos (Theocritus), the traditionally used Latin transliterations are provided. In the notes, as opposed to the poems, I have *tended* to use the Latinized names, again for the convenience of the reader who wishes to pursue further research. In addition, the name as it appears in the poem is listed first, then the alternate spelling, whether Greek or Latin, is offered in parentheses; the name as it is spelled in the poem is used throughout the rest of the note. Therefore, for the sake of consistency, if Kleopatra is mentioned in a poem, the spelling I use in the note begins with *K*, but if the note deals with her and she is not mentioned in the poem, I begin her name with *C*. It is my hope that with each subsequent translation from the Greek, the Hellenic names will become more familiar, and hence more the norm.

NOTES
by Aliki Barnstone and Willis Barnstone

The first date given is the year of probable composition, the second date refers to its first publication, either in pamphlet form or in Cavafy's various collections: Poems 1908–1914 *(1920),* Poems 1907–1915 *(1926), and* Poems 1905– 1915 *(1930). We followed the dating established by Cavafy's editor, George Savidis.*

JULIAN AT THE MYSTERIES

Written 1896, with the title "Julian at Eleusis," unpublished.

Julian is the Latin name of the emperor's Greek name, which is Ioulianos. The usual name for Julian is "Julian the Apostate," because of his defection back to his Platonist and theurgic (magic) education. Born in Constantinople, the nephew of Constantine the Great (Megas Konstantinos), Julian ruled as emperor from 361 to 363. His reign was characterized by tolerance at a time when Christianity itself was torn between Orthodoxy (also called Trinitarianism), which would very slowly triumph, and Arianism. The dilemma concerned the nature of Jesus: whether Jesus was a human being with a divine soul, as the Orthodox maintained, or whether, according to the Arian Monophysitic view, God had created a divine figure who was not a human yet was not God himself.

At the Council of Nicaea in 325, the first ecumenical council, convened by and overseen by Constantine himself, Arianism was decreed a heresy and Bishop Arius was banned from Constantinople. The bishop fled to Alexandria. However, when Constantine, the first Christian emperor of the Roman Empire, was dying, on his last day of life he decided to put aside his own pagan background completely and become baptized as a true Christian. To the surprise of all, he summoned to his deathbed not an Orthodox priest but an Arian bishop, who by his orders baptized him as an Arian Christian. Needless to say, the forces pro and contra Arianism and questions as to the true Christological nature of Christ's person and deeds were fiercely disputed. Did Jesus have two natures, human and divine, as the Orthodox believed, or one divine state as the Monophysites contended? What was the meaning of the crucifixion, that is, was Jesus a suffering human being or a Monophysitic phantom of God? All these unresolved questions of faith and dogma continued to torment early Christianity. Though Arianism per se has not survived in the modern era, aspects of its theology have. For example, many Christians believe in the historical Jesus as a spiritual and moral teacher, but they do not believe in his divinity, that is, in the Holy Trinity.

Julian acted broad-mindedly with regard to both Christological factions, issuing edicts of tolerance. Furthermore, by returning to his pagan philosophical and Platonic training, he circumvented divisive matters of heresy. In 312 C.E., his uncle Constantine had converted to Christianity when in midbattle he had a vision of a flaming cross in the sky inscribed with the words, *"In hoc signo vinces"* ("By this sign you will conquer"). Julian returned to Constantine's original family religion, and became a pagan. Moreover, he attempted to turn the empire itself back to paganism.

After Constantine's death in 337, Constantine's sons, Constantine II, Constantius I, and Constans I (Konstantinos II, Konstantios II, and Konstans I) met and defied Constantine the Great's decree that the empire be divided between his sons and nephews. All the other princes of royal blood were executed, except for Gallus (Gallos) and Julian, who were young children. The empire was divided between Constantine II (who ruled the West, including Gaul, Spain, and Britain), Constantius (who ruled the East, excluding Thrace, Achaea, and Macedonia), and Constans (who ruled Africa, Illricum, Macedonia, and Achaea). In 340, Constantine II invaded Italy and died in an ambush, and Constans gained his brother's territory. Constans was himself assassinated by Magnentius's forces in 350, leaving Constantius as the sole emperor of a now united empire.

Constantius called Julian back from his scholarly retreat in Cappadocia in 351. In 354, convinced his nephew Gallus (Julian's half brother) was not a true Christian believer, he put him to death, leaving Julian as a more probable successor to the throne. Constantius was a fervent Arianist until his death, which further confused and deepened the divisions between Orthodox and Arianist factions of the clergy and their followers with respect to the essential dogmas of Christianity. With regard to military matters, he sent his cousin Julian on an unexpectedly successful military mission in Gaul to put down regional revolts by the Franks and Alemanni. By 360 Constantius began to distrust Julian, who was popular with the military commanders and troops, and he ordered his cousin into difficult combat with the Persians. In the course of battle Constantius's soldiers revolted against their sovereign, declaring Julian their true emperor. Julian accepted the soldiers' mandate. Constantius was resistant because he wanted to hold on to the western provinces, a move that would have split the empire again. Just as the two contenders were to go to battle with each other, Constantius fell sick. Before he died, he appointed Julian his successor.

When Julian became emperor he permitted all spiritual factions to function, but he openly used his authority to encourage a return to paganism. He did not permit Christians to teach classical philosophy and worked to restore the worship of the pagan gods. In his personal conduct, Julian was austere in his comportment to the point of prudishness. Of a modest and astringent character and of calm authority, he was absolutely distinct from the all too common rapacious and corrupt leaders and he did not succumb to persecuting opponents. Intellectually, he was broadly interested in classical philosophy, studied theurgic healing and Egyptian cosmological mysticism, and was fascinated by the early mystery rites at Eleusis (Elevsis). He knew both the Gnostic body-and-spirit dualism in Hermes Trismegistus and the transcendental oneness in Plotinus. Specifically, he installed the pagan philosopher Maximus of Ephesus (Efesos) (died 370 C.E.) in his court as a counselor. The bishop of Nikomedia was his official court religious advisor. Julian was a benevolent lawmaker and an accomplished writer. Many letters and a number of his books, which are basically critiques of Christian decadence, have survived. He was respected, if mistrusted, by the religious establishment, despite his decrees of religious open-mindedness. It is impossible to know what would have been the fate and development of late Christianity had the emperor of the Roman empire not been struck down at the age of thirty-two in a minor battlefield skirmish.

Cavafy's "Julian at the Mysteries" is the earliest of seven poems about Julian the Apostate. The poem was unpublished during his lifetime. The story the poem tells appears in Gibbons's *Decline and Fall of the Roman Empire*, which is almost certainly the poem's direct source.

For more on Julian see "Julian Seeing Indifference," "Julian in Nikomedia," "A Grand Procession of Priests and Laymen," "Julian and the Antiochians," "You Did Not Know," and "In the Suburbs of Antioch."

WALLS

Written 1896, and printed, presumably in final form, in 1897.

Savidis notes that the poem was printed in a private pamphlet, with the epigraph, "How do I suffer unjust things," from Aeschylus's *Prometheus Bound.*

AN OLD MAN

Written 1894, it was printed in a private pamphlet in 1897, and listed under the section heading "Fleeting Years," taken from Horace's "Oh, the fleeting [years]," *Odes,* II.14.

THE HORSES OF ACHILLES

Written 1896, printed 1897, and listed under the heading "Ancient Days."

Achilles' horses were Balius (Valios) and Xanthos (Xanthus), who were the offspring of Zefyros (Zephyr), the West Wind, and the harpy Podarge. Patroklos was Achilles' close young friend and lover. When he was killed by the Trojan hero Hector, Achilles was so enraged that he killed Hector in revenge and dragged his body back to the Greek camp. The story appears in the *Iliad,* XVI, ll. 149–54 and XVII, ll. 426–47.

For more on Patroklos, see "The Funeral of Sarpedon." For Achilles see "Disloyalty" and "Trojans." For Thetis see "Interruption" and "Disloyalty."

PRAYER

Written 1896, published 1898.

THE FUNERAL OF SARPEDON

Probably written 1892, printed in 1898, Cavafy rewrote it in 1908, the year of its publication. Cavafy considered the poem to be a poem from 1898. The poem is adapted from the *Iliad,* XVI, ll. 462–501, 666–84.

Sarpedon, son of Zeus and Laodameia, was the king of Lykia (Lycia), and an ally of the Trojans. Achilles' friend Patroklos (Patroclus) killed Sarpedon.

For more on Patroklos, see "The Horses of Achilles." For Apollo see "Disloyalty," "A Byzantine Nobleman in Exile Composing Verses," "Myris: Alexandria, 340 C.E.," and "In the Suburbs of Antioch."

CANDLES

Written 1893, published 1899. The poem was listed under the heading "Fleeting Years."

THE FIRST STEP

Written 1895, with the original title "The Last Step," and listed under "Our Art," published 1899.

Theokritos (Theocritus), born ca. 310 B.C.E. in Syracuse, is the father of pastoral poetry, a sophisticated city-dweller's perception of shepherd life in idealized nature. Theokritos wrote idylls, which served as a model for Virgil's *Bucolics* in which the eclogues create an imaginary Arcadia. The celebration of the pastoral deeply influenced Renaissance poetry, painting, and music, and persists in Beethoven's *Pastoral Symphony* and Picasso's Greek drawings. Cavafy's Theokritos is a re-creation. The poet Evmenis (Eumenes) is Cavafy's invention (and not to be confused with the well-known Macedonian general Evmenis under Alexander the Great [Megas Alexandros]).

WHEN THE WATCHMAN SAW THE LIGHT

Written 1900, unpublished.

The poem is taken from the prologue of Aeschylus's *Agamemnon* (458 B.C.E.), the first play of the *Oresteia* trilogy. King Atreus is the father of Agamemnon and Menelaus. The watchman sees the symbolic fire on Mount Arachnaion, which signifies the end of the Trojan War and Agamemnon's return. Upon his homecoming, he will be murdered by his wife Clytemnestra for having sacrificed their daughter, Iphigenia, to the goddess Artemis. The omen of the light also signals the next tragedy that will befall the cursed House of Atreus.

THE ENEMIES

Written 1900, unpublished.

CHE FECE . . . IL GRAN RIFIUTO

Written 1899, published 1901.

The title is from Dante's *Inferno*, Canto 3.60: "After I had recognized some

213

of them, / I saw and knew the shame of him who / through cowardice, made the great refusal." The poem refers to Celestine who became pope in 1294 and abdicated five months later, saying the great "No." Dante sees this as an act of cowardice, Cavafy as one of honor.

THE SOULS OF OLD MEN

Written 1898, listed under "Prisons," and published 1901.

INTERRUPTION

Written 1900, published 1901.

Metaneira, queen of Eleusis (Elevsis), and Peleus, king of Phthia, each intervened at a crucial moment. Metaneira asked the earth goddess Demeter (Dimitra) to perform a ritual of putting the baby Demophon (Demofon) in fire to make him immortal, that is, to burn off the mortal part of him, but, being frightened that her child might die in the fire, the queen interrupted the ceremony and Demophon was mortal. Similarly, Peleus, who married the sea goddess Thetis, asked Thetis to perform the fire ritual on Achilles, but, like Queen Metaneira, he became frightened, and interrupted the ritual, preventing Thetis from making Achilles immortal. As in many myths, there are several versions of the story, including the one in which Achilles is dipped in immortal waters, except for his heel, by which he was held.

For more on Thetis, see "Disloyalty."

THE WINDOWS

Written 1897, listed under "Prisons," and published 1903.

THERMOPYLAE

Written 1901, published 1903.

The Battle of Thermopylae took place in 480 B.C.E at a small pass between mountains and sea in Thessaly. The Persians (the Medes) were on their way to attack Athens when the Spartan king Leonidas defended the pass at Thermopylae (meaning "hot gates"), which was on the main north-south route to Athens. Six or seven thousand Greeks gathered there to stop a Persian army of a hundred thousand soldiers. A local Greek, Efialtis (Ephialtes), guided the Persians to attack the Greek defenses from the rear. When the Greeks discovered the treachery, the main army retreated, but Leonidas and a small Spartan force of three hundred stayed on to delay the enemy, refusing to surrender. They were annihilated, but the Greeks were able to regroup and save Athens. Of those who stayed, the poet Simonides wrote a famous epigraph: "Stranger, go back to Sparta and tell our people / that we who were slain obeyed the code."

Growing Strong

Written 1903, unpublished.

September, 1903

Written 1904, unpublished.

December, 1903

Written 1904, unpublished.

January, 1904

Written 1904, unpublished.

On the Stairs

Written 1904, unpublished.

At the Theater

Written 1904, unpublished.

Disloyalty

Written 1903, published 1904.

For more, see "The Horses of Achilles," "The Funeral of Sarpedon," and "Interruption."

WAITING FOR THE BARBARIANS

Written 1898, published in a private pamphlet in 1904.

In a comment on the poem, Cavafy writes that as the barbarians are a symbol, so, too, "the emperor, the senators, and the orators are not necessarily Roman." This influential poem has been used as an extended metaphor by many authors, including the Nobel laureate J. M. Coetzee, whose *Waiting for the Barbarians* (1982) won him the Booker Prize.

VOICES

Written 1894 under the title "Sweet Voices." Published 1894, rewritten in 1903, and published again in 1904.

DESIRES

Written 1904, published 1904.

TROJANS

Written 1900, published 1905.

The king of the Trojans is Priamos (Priam), his wife and queen is Ekavi (Hecuba).

For more on the Trojans, see "The Horses of Achilles."

KING DIMITRIOS

Written 1900, published 1906.

Dimitrios I of Macedonia (336–283 B.C.E.), was called the "Besieger of Cities" and also Sotir ("savior"). He became king of Macedonia in 299 after murdering Alexander V. In a major battle his troops went over to the enemy, King Pyrros of Epirus, leading to his defeat and the tale of his departure. The story of the poem is from Plutarch's *Life of Dimitrios,* XLIV and XLI, and from Lucian's *Dialogue,* "The Cock" found in *Lucian,* Loeb Classics, vol. 2, p. 227. See "On the March to Sinopi" for another historical poem based on Dimitrios's life.

Antony's Ending

Written 1907, unpublished.

The lady is Cleopatra (Kleopatra).

Savidis notes that the poem is "directly derived" from Shakespeare's *Antony and Cleopatra*, IV, xv.

For more on Antony, see "The God Abandons Antony," "In Alexandria, 31 B.C.E.," and "In a Township in Asia Minor."

The Procession of Dionysos

Written 1903, published 1907.

The anonymous king is probably the tyrant Hieron II of Syracuse in 270 B.C.E. The scene and the person of Damon are imaginary. The god Dionysos was especially venerated in Athens and Piraeus. A talent of silver or gold weighed approximately fifty-two pounds.

Hidden Things

Written 1908, unpublished.

Monotony

Written 1898. Original title was "Like the Past." Published 1908.

This Is the Man

Written 1898, published 1909.

Refers to a passage from *A Dream* by Lucian (Loukianos), in which the writer tells how he chose his literary career. The writer promises the young man that if he chooses to be a writer, at home or abroad, all will recognize him and say, "This is the man." Edessa was the capital of Osroini in Mesopotamia.

For more on Osroini, see "In a City of Osroini."

The Footsteps

Written 1893, with title "The Footsteps of the Eumenides," published 1897 under the listing "Ancient Days." Rewritten 1908 and published 1909.

The story of Nero Claudius Caesar (37–68 C.E.) is based on Suetonius in *Life of Nero*, XLVI. Nero was the son of Domitius Aenobarbus and Agrippina Junior. Agrippina married the Emperor Claudius, whom she persuaded to adopt her son Nero, who became emperor in 54. She poisoned Claudius in 55 to ensure that her son would remain as emperor. Nero had earlier poisoned his rival, Claudius's son, Britannicus. Then Nero murdered his mother in 59 and, three years later, his wife, Octavia. When half of Rome burned in 64, Nero accused the Christians of starting the fire and began the first Roman persecution.

The *Lares Familiares* were minor Roman deities that protected the household, who assumed the form of little statues placed on the hearth shrine called *Larium*.

The Furies were about to punish Nero for matricide and the murder of others in his immediate family.

See "Nero's Term" for more on his life and death.

The City

Written 1894 with the title "Once More in the Same City," and listed under "Prisons." It was published in 1910.

The Satrapy

Written 1903, probably rewritten 1905, and first published in the magazine *Nea Zoe* ("New Life") in 1909, and in collection form in 1910.

Cavafy wrote a letter in English to a friend, Periklis Anastasiadis, with intricate comments on the poem's prosody, except the conclusion. He wrote, "To a sympathetic reader—sympathetic by culture—who will think over the poem for a minute or two, my lines, I am convinced, will suggest an image of the deep, the endless 'désespérance,' which they contain 'yet cannot all reveal.' "

The Persian Empire was divided territorially into satrapies or provinces, each of which was governed by a satrap in the service of the monarchy. Artaxerxes became king of Persia in 464 B.C.E., at the death of his father Xerxes.

Susa, originally the capital of the kingdom of Elam (or Susiana) became, under Dareios I (521–486 B.C.E.), the capital of the Achaemenid Persian dynasty, in which Dareios, the grandfather of Artaxerxes, constructed palaces and a great elaborate gate inscribed with cuneiform scripts. In the Torah (Old Testament), Susa is Shushan, "city of lilies," from which the Hebrew name Shusana and English Susan derive, meaning "lilies." The fourth-millennium city and the Elamite Empire, mentioned in Isaiah and Jeremiah, was a major force until its conquest by Babylonia in the second millennium, and its eventual absorption into the Persian Empire.

The story in the poem is invented, though it is placed in a historical context. Cavafy notes that the anonymous speaker is not one of the great political refugees received at the court but an artist or scientist.

THE IDES OF MARCH

Written 1906, published 1911.

Artemidoros was a Greek philosopher in Rome and a friend of Julius Caesar. He is mentioned in Plutarch's *Life of Caesar* and in Suetonius's *Julius Caesar*. He tried in vain to hand Caesar a message concerning the plot by Brutus and Cassius to murder him. Earlier Caesar had been warned by a soothsayer. (See "Theodotos.") In 44 B.C.E. on the Ides of March, Julius Caesar was stabbed to death in the Senate house by his closest friends, Brutus and Cassius. In Latin "Ides" refers to the fifteenth day of March, May, July, or October or the thirteenth day in any other month in the ancient Roman calendar.

FINISHED

Written 1910, published 1911.

A SCULPTOR FROM TYANA

Written 1893, with the title "A Sculptor's Studio," rewritten in 1903, published 1911.

Tyana was a city in Cappadocia and birthplace of the philosopher Apollonios.

Rhea was a Titan, the sister and wife of Kronos, with whom she had Zeus,

Poseidon, Hades (Pluto), Hestia, Hera, and Demeter (Dimitra). She helped Zeus overthrow Kronos. She is the great mother goddess.

Pompey (106–48 B.C.E.) was a Roman general and rival of Julius Caesar, later defeated by Caesar at Pharsala and murdered in Egypt.

Marius (d. 269 C.E.) was the second Roman emperor of the so-called "Gallic Empire," whose short reign lasted between two days and twelve weeks. He rose to power when the first emperor of the Gallic Empire, Postumus, was murdered by his own troops for not permitting them to sack Moguntiacum (Mainz), the capital of Germania Superior.

Paulus Aemilius (ca. 229–160 B.C.E.) was a Roman general who sacked Epirus and set up Roman dominions in Greece.

Scipio Africanus Major (Publicus Cornelius) (235–ca. 183 B.C.E.) was a Roman consul and general who invaded and defeated Carthage and ended the Punic War by defeating Hannibal at Zama (202 B.C.E.).

THE GOD ABANDONS ANTONY

Written 1910, published 1911.

Antony (Marcus Antonius) (83?–30 B.C.E.) was a Roman orator, politician, and leader of the empire, one of the ruling triumvirate consisting of Octavian (later Caesar Augustus), Lepidus, and Antony himself, the orator with the golden tongue. The alliance fell apart because of Antony's liaison with Cleopatra (Kleopatra), queen of Egypt, and his residence in Alexandria as head of a southern Roman Empire. Octavian defeated Antony and Cleopatra's armies at the sea battle off Actium. On the evening before Antony's foreseen defeat at the gates of Alexandria by Octavian's invading armies, which will result in Antony's suicide, the sounds of a mysterious troupe of musicians and other revelers are heard in the street passing below his window. They disappear at the nearest gates of the enemy, and this is considered a sign that Dionysos, the god who Antony believed was his protector, now has abandoned him. This scene is recounted in Plutarch's *Life of Antony*, 75, which serves as the basis for Cavafy's poem as well as Shakespeare's *Antony and Cleopatra*.

For more on Antony, see "Antony's Ending," "In Alexandria, 31 B.C.E.," and "In a Township in Asia Minor."

IONIAN

Written 1886 with the title "Memory," published in 1896; rewritten in 1905 with the title "Thessaly." Last version published in 1911.

THE GLORY OF THE PTOLEMIES

Written 1896, rewritten 1911, published 1911.

After Alexander the Great (Megas Alexandros) (356–323 B.C.E.) died, his generals divided up the territories Alexander had conquered. The Ptolemies (Lagids) were fifteen Macedonian kings in Egypt whose reign lasted from 323 to 30 B.C.E. They ruled from Alexandria, a city founded by Alexander in 332. The Seleucids (Selefkids) were a dynasty descended from Seleucius Nicator (Selefkis Nikator), Alexander's friend, who became king of the Eastern provinces, which included the cities of Antioch in Syria and Seleucia (Selefkia) in Mesopotamia (Iraq). The Seleucid dynasty reigned for two centuries in which Hellenistic art, a hybrid of the Greek and Near Eastern traditions, flourished. Cavafy does not specify which Lagidis (Ptolemy) or Seleucid is portrayed in the poem.

For more about Ptolemies and the Seleucids, see "Philhellene," "Alexandrian Kings," "Theodotos," "Orofernis," "The Battle of Magnesia," "The Displeasure of the Selefkid," "One of Their Gods," "Kaisarion," "Envoys from Alexandria," "Of Dimitrios Sotir (162–150 B.C.E.)," "A Craftsman of Wine Bowls," "Those Who Fought for the Achaian League," "To Antiohos Epifanis," "The Priest of Serapeion," "A Grand Procession of Priests and Laymen," "In Sparta," and "They Should Have Cared."

ITHAKA

A distinct version, "Second Odyssey," was written in 1894, but remained unpublished until 1985. The present version was written in 1910, published in 1911.

In Homer's *Odyssey*, the Laistrygonians and the Cyclops were fierce, man-eating giants whom Odysseus encountered on his way back to Ithaka.

At Jacqueline Kennedy Onassis's request, "Ithaka" was read at her funeral.

On Hearing of Love

Written 1911, unpublished.

The Dangers

Published 1911.

Myrtias is an invented character.

Emperor Konstans and Emperor Konstantios II were brothers who ruled jointly (337–350 C.E.) after the death of their father, Constantine the Great (Megas Konstantinos), the first Christian emperor of the Roman Empire (285?–337 C.E.). In 340 the brothers went to war with each other and Konstantinos was killed. Konstans ruled until 350, when he was killed by one of his soldiers.

For more on Constantine the Great and his sons, see "Julian in Nikomedia."

Philhellene

Written 1906, published 1912.

In Hellenistic times it was common for non-Greek but Hellenizing rulers to add the title "Philhellene" (lover of Greek things) to their surnames. It appears that the protagonist here is a minor monarch of the Seleucid (Selefkid) kingdom, who is enhancing his image by engraving his face on a new coin.

Zagros remains the name of a mountain range in Persia, dividing Media from Assyria and Elam (Susiana).

Phraata was a city in Media, a non-Persian kingdom in western Persia, which conquered the Persian Empire but also merged with it. The Medes in literature, and even in history, were often used as a synonym for Persians. At the time of the poem, during the Seleucid period, the city of Media was a winter residence of the Parthian kings. Parthia formed another independent part of the greater Persian Empire between Afghanistan and the Indus Valley. There was a constant changing of borders and mingling of peoples in this huge area.

Herodis Attikos

Written 1900, rewritten 1911, published 1912.

Herodis Attikos (Herod of Attica) (101–177 C.E.) was a rich Athenian, a well-known sophist, and friend of the Roman emperor Hadrian and the philosopher

Marcus Aurelius. Alexandros of Selefkia (Alexander of Seleucia) was "a clay Plato," as Philostratos calls him in *Lives of the Sophists*, II B, 1–15 and E, I.

ALEXANDRIAN KINGS

Written 1912, published 1912.

Kleopatra's (Cleopatra's) son Kaisarion (Caesarion) was executed at fourteen by Octavian, and his half brothers, the youngest of whom was two years old, Alexandros (Alexander) and Ptolemaios Filadelfos (Ptolemy Philadelphus), were taken to Rome as hostages. Caesarion was fathered by Julius Caesar, his younger half brothers by Antony. The ceremony proclaiming the brothers kings was orchestrated by Antony. Four years later, Antony and Cleopatra committed suicide. See Plutarch's *Life of Antony*, LIV, and Shakespeare's *Antony and Cleopatra*, III, vi.

For more, see "Kaisarion."

COME BACK

Written 1904 with the title "Sensual Memory," rewritten 1909, published 1912.

IN CHURCH

Written 1892, rewritten 1901 and 1906, probably printed 1912.

VERY RARELY

Written 1911, published 1913.

AS MUCH AS YOU CAN

Written 1905 with the title "A Life," published 1913.

FOR THE SHOP

Written 1912, published 1913.

I WENT

Written 1905, published 1913.

"I Will Tell the Rest to Those Down in Hades"

Written 1913, unpublished.

Like This

Written 1913, unpublished.

Exiles

Written 1914, unpublished.
    The speaker is invented, but the narration is historical. The poem is set in Alexandria after its conquest by the Arabs in 641 C.E. See "Imenos."
    After 867 C.E. the exiles, who are loyal to Michael III and to Photius, hope that the emperor Vassilios I (Basil I) will be toppled because he seized the throne from Michael III, whom he had assassinated. In the same year Vassilios also deposed Photius, the Patriarch of Constantinople.
    Nonnos the Panopolitan is an Egyptian Greek poet (c. 450–470 B.C.E.).

The Tomb of Lysias the Grammarian

Written 1911, published 1914.
    Lysias is an invented character.

The Tomb of Evrion

Written 1912, published 1914.
    The name Evrion contains the ancient and modern Greek word for Jew ("Evraios," a "Hebrew"). In classical Alexandria, the Jews were a sizable percentage of the population and represented a major concentration of Jews. At this time, the Jews were perhaps ten percent of the peoples in the Roman Empire. The references to Evrion's being learned allude to the Alexandrian Jewish scholarly tradition. Philo the Judaeus was a major Platonist philosopher, and gave the notion of four ladder steps of mystical transport to ultimate adhesion with God, which became the basis for Plotinus and later meditation in Sufi and Judeo-Christian traditions. Also in Alexandria, the Jews translated the Old Testament into Greek in the second century B.C.E. for Jews who could no longer read the Scriptures in the original Hebrew. This is the famous Septuagint Bible. Cavafy writes frequently about the Jews

of Alexandrian antiquity, feeling kinship, recognizing fellow outsiders. We see this in "Of the Jews," to speak of the conflict in ethical and emotional loyalties between Jews and Christians on the one hand and classical pagan ideals on the other. See other examples of Greco-Jewish poems in "Aristovoulos," "Of the Jews (50 C.E.), and "Alexandros Iannaios and Alexandra."

Arsinoitis, an area of the city of Arsinoe in the Fayum in Egypt, was built on the ruins of Krokodeilopolis by Ptolemy Philadelphus (Ptolemaios Filadelfos), to honor his wife, Arsinoe II.

CHANDELIER

Written 1895, published 1914.

FAR OFF

Written 1914, published 1914.

THE WISE SENSE WHAT IS TO COME

Written 1896, with the title "Imminent Things," published 1899. Final version 1915.

THEODOTOS

Written 1911, perhaps with the title "Victory," published 1915.

The orator Theodotos was from Chios (Hios) or Samos. He was the teacher of Ptolemy XII (Ptolemaios XII) and persuaded the Egyptians to kill Pompey when he landed after he was defeated in Egypt by Caesar. There is no historical document that suggests that Theodotos brought Caesar Pompey's head.

AT THE CAFÉ DOOR

Probably written 1904, with the title "From the Hands of Eros," printed 1915.

HE SWEARS

Written 1905, with the title "Libidinousness," printed 1915.

As I Lounged and Lay on Their Beds

Written 1915, unpublished.

One Night

Written 1915, with the title "One of My Evenings," and later as "One of My Nights," printed 1915.

Morning Sea

Printed 1915.

Drawn

Written 1914, printed 1915.

Orofernis

Written 1904, printed 1916.

Cappadocia is in east central Turkey. Orofernis (Orophernes) was the son of Ariarathis IV (Ariathes IV), a Hellenized Persian king of Cappadocia (220–163 B.C.E.). His mother Antiohida (Antiochida) was the daughter of Antiochus III (Antiohos III) the Great; his grandmother was Stratoniki (Stratonice). Dimitrios is Dimitrios Sotir ("Savior") of Syria (187–150 B.C.E.), who was responsible for making Orofernis king in 157. But his brother Ariarathis V ousted him three years later. Orofernis went into exile in Antioch, and his last move was his attempt to take the throne of Sotir, his protector, but in this he also failed. He died in 154 B.C.E.

For more on Antiochus, see "The Battle of Magnesia."

For more on Dimitrios Sotir, see "The Displeasure of the Selefkid" and "Of Dimitrios Sotir (162–150 B.C.E.)."

The Battle of Magnesia

Written 1913, printed probably 1916.

Philip V (Filippos V) was the last independent king of Macedonia. He was defeated by the Romans at the battle of Cynoscephalae in Thessaly in 197 B.C.E. Antiochus III (Antiohos III), normally an ally, did not come to his aid.

The scene is seven years later, after the battle of Magnesia, northeast of Smyrna, where the Roman Scipio brothers defeated the Seleucid (Selefkid) king, which established Roman rule in the Hellenized East. After the defeat, his son Antiochus IV (Antiohos IV), who still claimed to be king of greater Syria, was taken to Rome as a hostage. He later was permitted to invade Judea, where he attempted to extirpate Judaism. He failed in his battles with the Maccabees, and Judea was liberated from Syrian rule, which is celebrated by the Feast of Hanukkah. After the diverse disgraces of Antiochus III, Philip, despite his terrible defeat, collaborated with the Romans, as he had earlier collaborated with Antiochus the Great, all the time attempting to rebuild his own kingdom. Cavafy himself was aware of the historical Philip, whose apparent weariness was not to be believed. In the Keeley and Sherrard translations, Savidis notes, "According to one of Cavafy's oral comments, Philip's lassitude is a sham, concealing his preparation for a new attack against the Romans" (C. P. Cavafy, *Collected Poems*, p. 223).

MANUEL KOMNINOS

Written 1905, probably printed 1916.

Manuel I Komninos (Manuel I Comnenus) was emperor of Byzantium (1143–1180 C.E.). One of six Komninos emperors, Manuel fought many battles, against the Turks of Iconium, the Hungarians, and the Normans of Italy. However, he was defeated disastrously at Myriokephalon in 1174, which weakened the empire. The Orthodox Church disapproved of his often good relations with Rome, as well as his endless lechery, for which he was renowned. When he was dying, he shed his royal garments for the robes of a monk. Cavafy seizes on a telling moment of the monarch's life, placing in perspective the warrior-emperor's disbelief in the chattering astrologers, his radical assumption of monk's habits, and the disquieting happiness of his last display of modesty as he dresses in his faith.

THE DISPLEASURE OF THE SELEFKID

Written 1910, probably printed 1916.

Dimitrios Selefkidis Sotir (Savior) (187–150 B.C.E.), who was the son of Seleucid IV Philopator (Selefkos IV Filopatros) (218–174 B.C.E.), and grandson of Antiochus (Antiohos) the Great, became the king of Syria.

However, with the skirmishes between the Roman and Seleucid (Selefkid) Empires, Rome held Dimitrios hostage for sixteen years (178–162). While in Rome, Ptolemy VI Philometor (Ptolemaios VI Filomitor), in exile from Alexandria, arrives in Italy, in shabby clothes, to supplicate the Roman authorities to restore his kingship, which his brother, Ptolemy VIII Euergetis (Ptolemaios VIII Evergetis) (see "They Should Have Cared"), has taken from him (see "Envoys from Alexandria").

See "Orofernis" and "Of Dimitrios Sotir (162–150 B.C.E.)."

When They Are Aroused

Written 1913, printed 1916.

In the Street

Written in 1913, printed 1916.

Before the Statue of Endymion

Written 1895, printed 1916.

Endymion was a young mythological shepherd known for his beauty. In one version of the myth, Endymion, in his vanity, asked Zeus to keep him in eternal sleep to preserve his youth and beauty. Then Selene, the moon goddess saw him sleeping naked on Mount Latmos near Miletos (on the coast south of Ephesus) and fell in love with him. In another version, Selene saw the naked beauty and fell in love with the shepherd and persuaded Zeus to let her keep him in eternal sleep so as to preserve his beauty, so she could visit him every night. Latmos was also held by some to be one of his tombs.

In a City of Osroini

Written 1916, with the title "Charmides," printed 1917.

Osroini was a kingdom in Mesopotamia, whose capital was Edessa. Charmides was Plato's uncle, who was killed in a duel. Plato has a dialogue bearing his name. In it, Socrates is inspired by the extreme beauty of the young man and discusses wisdom as the knowledge of good and evil.

For more on Osroini, see "This Is the Man."

Passing Through

Written 1916, printed 1917.

For Ammonis, Who Died at Twenty-nine, in 610

Written 1915, with the title "Epitaph for the Poet Ammonis," published 1917.
    Both characters are imaginary. Savidis notes that the name Ammonis is Egyptian and the name Raphael is Coptic. The year 610 is the year that Mohammed began to spread the teachings he had received from the angel Gabriel. Mohammed was resting in a cave when Gabriel began to "recite" to him the word of God. That recitation became the Koran, which means "recitation."

One of Their Gods

Written 1899, with the title "One of Them," printed 1917.
    Selefkia (Seleucia) is the name of between ten and twelve cities in the Seleucid Empire, of which Selefkia on the Tigris was the most resplendent and famous. It was founded around 312 B.C.E. by Seleucus I Nicator (Selefkos I Nikator), and was the capital of his empire.

Evening

Written 1916, with the title "Alexandrian," printed 1917.

Sensual Pleasure

Written 1913, printed 1917.

Gray

Written 1917, published 1917.

The Tomb of Iasis

Written 1917, published 1917.
    Iasis is an imaginary figure.
    Narcissus (Narkissos is from Greek *narke*, "numb" as in "narcotic") was

the son of the river god Kefissos. He was a youth known for his beauty and vanity. Because of his indifference to Echo's love, Aphrodite made him fall in love with his own image in a pool; he drowned as he attempted to embrace his own image. He was transformed into a flower of the same name. In another version Aphrodite makes him waste away because of his rejection of Echo, and he falls into the pool.

Hermes was a herald or messenger of the gods, and also known for commerce, cunning, invention, and theft.

IN THE MONTH OF ATHYR

Written 1917, published 1917.

In the ancient Egyptian calendar Athyr corresponds to October–November and is the name of the goddess of the tomb and erotic love.

Kappa Zeta (K, Z) are Greek letters that numerically stand for twenty-seven.

I HAVE GAZED SO LONG—

Written 1916, with the title "For the Beautiful Things," published 1917.

THE TOMB OF IGNATIOS

Written 1916, with the title "Tomb of Hieronymos," printed 1917.

Ignatios, who was Kleon, was an invented figures.

HOUSE WITH GARDEN

Written 1917, unpublished.

DAYS OF 1903

Written 1907, with the title "March 1907," printed 1917.

HALF AN HOUR

Written 1917, unpublished.

The Tobacco Shop Window

Written 1907, with the title "The Closed Carriage," printed 1917.

Remember, Body . . .

Written 1916, published 1917 or 1918.

The Tomb of Lanis

Written 1916, published 1917 or 1918.
The characters are imaginary. The names represent the diversity of Alexandria: Lanis is Greek, Markos is Greek and Roman (Marcus), and Rametihos is Egyptian. "Kyrenian" refers to one from the major city of Kyrene (Cyrene) far to the east of Alexandria, which is now in Libya.

Hyacinth (Hyakinthos) was a mortal with whom Apollo fell in love. Zephyr (Zefyros) killed Hyacinth in a rage of jealousy, but a flower, bearing his name, sprang from his blood.

Meaning

Written 1915, published 1917 or 1918.

Kaisarion

Written 1917, with the title "Of Ptolemy Caesar," printed 1918
Kaisarion (Caesarion), born in 47 B.C.E., was the son of Kleopatra (Cleopatra) and presumably Julius Caesar. He was given the title "King of Kings" by Mark Antony. When Octavian, the future emperor Augustus, defeated Antony in 31 B.C.E., he ordered the execution of Kaisarion, who by his blood was a rival to Octavian himself. According to Plutarch in *Life of Antony,* Octavian consulted the Alexandrian philosopher Arrios, who advised the emperor, "Too many Caeasars is not good." This phrase is also found in the *Iliad,* II, l. 204: "It is not a good thing to have many kings."

When Cavafy praises the women, "all the Berenikis and Kleopatras," he is referring to the unusually powerful positions that the Ptolemy Queens held in the dynasty. The queens frequently co-ruled with their husbands, who were also often their brothers, or their sons. There were four named Arsinoe, four named Bereniki (Berenice), and seven named Kleopatra (Cleopatra).

For more on Kaisarion, see "Alexandrian Kings."

For more on Mark Antony, see "Antony's Ending," "The God Abandons Antony," and "In Alexandria, 31 B.C.E."

NERO'S TERM

Written 1915, with the title "Toward the Fall," published 1918.

Nero Claudius Caesar (37–68 C.E.) was emperor of the Roman Empire from 54 to 68. Nero was attracted to Greek arts, athletics, and music, and held festivals of the Greek arts in Rome and introduced Greek athletic contests to replace gladiatorial combat in the Coliseum. Galba, the Roman governor in Spain, was asked by the Senate to return to Rome and replace Nero, whom they had declared a public enemy. Galba was seventy-three years old. At the villa of a friend belonging to the freedman Phaon, on hearing the decision of his dethronement, Nero committed suicide.

See "Footsteps."

ENVOYS FROM ALEXANDRIA

Written 1915, published 1918.

This scene in Delphi was invented by Cavafy.

The rival Ptolemaic (Lagid) kings are Ptolemy VI Philometor (Ptolemaios VI Filomitor), and his brother, Ptolemy VIII Euergetes II (Ptolemaios VIII Evergetis II), who dispute the throne in 164 C.E. Euergetes exiled Philometor, who went to Rome to plead his case. The decision in Rome was favorable to him and he was restored as the monarch of Alexandria, while Euergetes II was given Cyrene (Kyrene), Libya, to rule.

For more details, see "The Displeasure of the Selefkid."

ARISTOVOULOS

Written 1916, published 1918.

The figures in this poem are Hasmoneans (also called Asmoneans), that is, descendants of the Maccabee brothers, who successfully fought Antiochus IV (Antiohos IV), the Seleucid (Selefkid) monarch of Syria. Antiochus attempted to exterminate Judaism in 166 B.C.E. He looted the Temple's treasures and desecrated it by sacrificing a pig on its holy altar and erecting a statue of Zeus inside it. After years of warfare, the Maccabees triumphed; that victory is celebrated as the Feast of Hannukah. Judaism was preserved, thereby making possible its later Abrahamic offsprings, Christianity and Islam.

The Hasmonean dynasty ruled Israel from 142 to 63 B.C.E. Herod the Great (?73–4 B.C.E.) became king in 40 B.C.E, and, in 37 B.C.E., by marrying Miriam, he united two feuding lines of the Hasmoneans. By the time of Herod and Aristovoulos, the Hasmoneans, as rulers, had become thoroughly Hellenized and their appointment to office was determined or approved by Rome. Herod's son Herod Antipas (died ca. 40 C.E.) was king or tetrarch of Israel when Pontius Pilate, according to the Gospels, sent Jesus before him for his judgment.

Hasmonean Aristovoulos III of Judea (Yehuda) and his sister, Miriam, were the children of Alexandra. Miriam was the wife of Herod I, the Great. Kypros (Cypros) was Herod's mother, Salome—who asked for John the Baptist's head—was Herod's sister. Aristovoulos, Herod's brother-in-law (his wife Miriam's brother), was a young man of famed beauty. His good looks came to the attention of Mark Antony. However, all this became irrelevant when, urged by Kypros and Salome, who wished to eliminate any possible future claims to the throne, Herod had the young Aristovoulos drowned in a pool. For extensive information, see Josephus's *Roman Antiquities*.

For more Greco-Jewish poems, see "The Tomb of Evrion," "Of the Jews (50 C.E.)," and "Alexandros Iannaios and Alexandra."

IN THE PORT

Written 1917, with the title "Tombs of Doros," published 1918.

AIMILIANOS MONAI, ALEXANDRIAN, 628–655 C.E.

Written 1898, with the title "Protected." Revised and printed 1918.

Aimilianos is an imaginary character. The date in the title suggests that the "evil men" who cause Aimilianos to leave Alexandria and go to Sicily are the Muslims, who conquered Alexandria in 641 C.E.

SINCE NINE O'CLOCK

Written 1917, with title "Half Past Twelve," printed 1918.

OUTSIDE THE HOUSE

Written 1917, printed probably 1919.

In the Greek edition of Cavafy's poems, *Τα Ποιήματα* (*The Poems*), edited by George Savidis, both "Outside the House" and "The Next Table" are listed in the contents as published in 1918. However, in the notes, Savidis states that the poems were probably printed in 1919. This discrepancy appears in both the Dalven and the Keeley and Sherrard translations. I chose 1919, since it is the probable date of publication.

THE NEXT TABLE

Written 1918, printed probably 1919.

For information about dating, see above, "Outside the House."

THE BANDAGED SHOULDER

Written 1919, unpublished.

THE AFTERNOON SUN

Written 1918, printed 1919.

IMENOS

Written 1915, with the title "Love It All the More," rewritten 1919, printed 1919.

Imenos is fictional. Michael III (842–867) was a Byzantine emperor. Apparently, Michael III is not the target of "the depraved time," but a good emperor who had to share power with Emperor Basil I, known for ruthlessly killing enemies or would-be enemies.

OF THE JEWS (50 C.E.)

Written 1912, printed 1919.

Ianthis is an imaginary character. A Jew with a Greek name, whose father's name is Roman, thereby reflecting the diverse elements in Alexandria. He lived during the reign of Claudius (41–54 C.E.), who restored many rights of the Jews, which is reflected in Ianthis's quandary of loyalty to Judaism and Greco-Roman culture.

For more Greco-Jewish poems, see "The Tomb of Evrion," "Aristovoulos," and "Alexandros Iannaios and Alexandra."

To Stay

Written 1918, printed 1919.

Of Dimitrios Sotir (162–150 B.C.E.)

Written 1915, printed 1919.

Dimitrios Sotir had the epithet "Savior" because he unseated the tyrant Irakleides (Herakleides). As a boy of nine he was sent to Rome as a hostage, where he remained until the age of twenty-five. The throne of Syria was occupied by his uncle Antiochus IV Epiphanes (Antiohos IV Epifanis) and by his young cousin Antiochus V (Antiohos V). At twenty-five he escaped, killed his cousin, and took the throne for himself. He fought against Ptolemy IV (Ptolemaios IV) of Egypt, put down a revolt in Babylonia, and attempted like his uncle Antiochus IV to conquer Israel. In 150 he was defeated in battle by a gathering of enemies and was ultimately killed by an adventurer and pretender to the throne, Alexandros Valas (Alexander Balas). So the poem ends with early and late enemies.

See "The Displeasure of the Selefkid," "Envoys from Alexandria," "The Favor of Alexandros Valas," "To Antiohos Epifanis," and "Epitaph of Antiohos, King of Kommagini."

On the Ship

Written 1919, with the title "The Ionian Sea," printed 1919.

If Truly Dead

Written 1897, with the title "Absence," rewritten 1910 and 1920, printed 1920.

Apollonios of Tyana, a first-century neo-Pythagorian philosopher from Cappadocia (4 B.C.E.–96 or 98 C.E.), was said to be a magician, miracle maker, and healer like Jesus and his contemporary Hasids in Galilee. He traveled as far as India. *Life of Apollonios of Tyana* by Flavius Philostratos, one of Cavafy's favorite books, appears to be based on memoirs by Damis, one of the philosopher's students.

The second part of the poem is by an imaginary pagan in the time of Emperor Justin I the Elder (ca. 482–565), a rude soldier and uncle of the great Justinian (483–565).

YOUNG MEN FROM SIDON (400 C.E.)

Written 1920, printed 1920.

Meleagros (Meleager) (140–70 B.C.E.) was a major Syrian poet who lived in Tyros and Sidon, Phoenicia (present-day Lebanon), who wrote epigrams and erotic poetry and collected the first anthology of epigrams and other poems. He also was highly educated, sophisticated, and spoke for an internationalization of Greek speech and culture in all Hellenistic lands. Krinagoras (first century B.C.E to about 11 C.E.) was an epigrammist from Mytilini. Rianos (b. 275 B.C.E.) was a scholar and poet from Crete. Of the great tragedians, Aeschylus seems to have been Cavafy's favorite and he left his mark in his poems, as in "When the Watchman Saw the Light." The cited passages in stanza three are by Aeschylus. These epitaphs say nothing about Aeschylus as a tragedian but only his role in the victory at the battle of Marathon against the Persians (490 B.C.E.). Datis and Artafernis were Persian leaders in the expedition that ended in defeat at Marathon.

SO THEY WILL COME

Printed 1920.

DAREIOS

Written perhaps before 1897, rewritten 1917, printed 1920.

The scene and the timid poet Fernazis, a Persian name, are fictional. Dareios was Dareios (Darius) the Great (521–486 B.C.E.). Among other achievements he defeated the Babylonians and ended the Babylonian Captivity of the Jews, sung so eloquently in the Psalms and in Jeremiah. His name in the West is best known for his defeat at Marathon, which saved Greek civilization.

The poem actually takes place in the city of Amisos, on the Pontos (Black

Sea) coast in 74 B.C.E., which was to fall to the Romans three years later. Mithridatis VI Evpator (Mithridates VI Eupator) was a partially Hellenized Persian king, who successfully fought the Romans. He originally ruled with his brother, whom he killed in 74 B.C.E. When he was defeated by a smaller Roman force, led by Lucullus and Pompey, his son, Pharnaces, overthrew him and forced suicide upon him. Cavafy roams between periods, casting all comments in the tongue of the poet Fernazis, who speculates wishfully.

ANNA KOMNINI

Written 1917, published 1920.

Anna Komnini (Comnena) (1083–1146 C.E.) was the daughter of Alexius I Commenus (Alexios I Komninos), the Byzantine emperor (1081–1118). She was one of the earliest women historians and a crucial writer in the Byzantine world. At her father's death she conspired to deprive her younger brother of the throne in favor of her husband, Nicephorus Byrennius (Nikiforos Vryennios). She failed. At his death in 1136/37, she withdrew to a convent where she wrote The Alexiad, which praises her father and is hostile to the Roman Church and the First Crusade during which they massacred Jews in Germany, intruded in Byzantine territory, were defeated by the Turks, and finally reached Jerusalem, the only crusade with partial success. The Byzantines were furious at all the crusades, which after several sackings of Constantinople, weakened the empire and made inevitable its ultimate fall in 1453. We see this first in the Alexiad, where the motives and sins of the crusaders are eloquently elaborated.

A BYZANTINE NOBLEMAN IN EXILE COMPOSING VERSES

Written 1921, printed 1921.

The scene seems to refer to the Byzantine emperor Michael VII, dethroned in 1078 by Nikiforos III Votaniatis (Nicephorus III Botaniates), who was then dethroned in 1081 by Alexius I Commenus (Alexios I Komninos), whose wife was Irini Doukas (1066–1123).

THEIR BEGINNING

Written 1915, printed 1921.

The Favor of Alexandros Valas

Written probably 1916, with the title "The Wheel of the Chariot," printed 1921.

Alexandros Valas (Alexander Balas), king of Syria (150–145 B.C.E.), the imposter, defeated Dimitrios Sotir and killed him to seize the throne. See "Of Dimitrios Sotir (162–150 B.C.E.)."

The Melancholy of Iason Kleandros, Poet in Kommagini, 595 C.E.

Written probably 1918, with the title "Knife," printed 1921.

Iason (Jason) Kleandros is an imaginary character in Kommagini, a small state northeast of Syria, on the western bank of the upper Euphrates, whose capital was Samosata. Like most states or provinces in this part of Asia Minor, it had many rulers. It went from Assyrian to Selefkid to Byzantine to Arab rule, with a period of independence from 164 B.C.E. to 72 C.E. After it was plundered by Hosroes I of Persia in 552, it became part of the Byzantine Empire until 638 C.E., when it was conquered by the Arabs. From the title, which gives the date 595 C.E., it is clear that Iason Kleandros (a Greek name) lived in the period when his state passed from Byzantine to Muslim rule, which is "the ghastly knife." Here Iason falls back on memory and poetry to numb the melancholy wound.

Dimaratos

Written 1904, rewritten 1911, printed 1921.

The conversation of Porfyry (Porphyry) (234–305 C.E.) is about a supposed sophistic essay in the fourth century B.C.E., which itself goes back to Persia ca. 480 B.C.E. Porfyry was a student of the greatest of the Neoplatonists, Plotinus (205–269/70 C.E.). A major scholar, editor, and philosopher, he is often cited for a question he is said to have asked Plotinus, "Would you like to have your picture painted?" Plotinus replied, "Why paint an illusion of an illusion?" The poem's central figure is colorful Dimaratos, who seems to be everywhere. He was king of Sparta from 510 to 491 B.C.E., reigning jointly with Kleomenis until Kleomenis and Leotihidis had the Delphic Oracle bribed to say that Dimaratos was not the legitimate heir to the throne. So Dimaratos resigned, Leotihidis assumed the throne, and

Dimaratos went over to the Persians, taking refuge in the court of King Dareios (Darius) the Great. He gave advice to the Persians in the sea and land battles, but felt uneasy for going over to the other side. He helped Xerxes against his old collaborator and enemy Leotihidis, and, as Cavafy makes clear at the end, knew that Leotihidis and the Greeks would triumph.

I Brought to Art

Written 1921, printed 1921.

From the School of the Celebrated Philosopher

Written 1921, printed 1921.

Ammonios Sakkas (died 243 C.E.), a philosopher who taught in Alexandria, was called the "Socrates of Neoplatonism." He was born a Christian or a Christian Gnostic, and went over to paganism, that is, classical philosophy in his youth. His own writings, if he did more than Platonic dialogue with his students, have not survived, but his students were at the center of the three competing belief systems: classical paganism, Christianity, and Gnosticism.

His two most famous students were the Neoplatonist Plotinos (205–269/70) and the Christian churchman and philosopher Origen (185–255). Origen was the first intellectual Christian to allegorize the Bible to make the Old Testament a prediction and confirmation of the New Testament (which was still in formation). Finally, the last of the famous students that Sakkas was said to have taught was the grammarian and literary theoretician Longinus, whose dates are unknown, but most often set in the first rather than the second century of the Common Era. The Alexandrian Longinus wrote, among other major works, *On the Sublime.*

A Craftsman of Wine Bowls

Written 1903, with the title "The Amphora," rewritten 1912, printed 1921.

The imaginary situation takes place when Irakleidis (Herakleidis) was the treasurer of Antiochus IV Epiphanes (Antiochos IV Epifanis) (215–164 B.C.E.). The battle of Magnesia took place in 189 B.C.E., and Antiochus III the Great failed to come to the aid of Philip V (238–179 B.C.E.), the last Macedonian king of that name, who was attempting to extend the

Macedonian influence by battling the Persian Selefkid Empire of Antiochus III. Selefkia (Seleucia) was south of Bagdad, corresponding largely to ancient Babylonia, and west of Iran or Persia proper. The nature of the Selefkids is confusingly mixed, since by this time the throne was ostensibly a Persian throne. However, the monarchs of Selefkia were either highly Hellenized Selefkid (Seleucid) Persians or Greeks or Macedonians, such as Philip V, who wished to extend Macedonian rule into Asia Minor.

For more details, see "The Battle of Magnesia," "Of Dimitrios Sotir (162–150 B.C.E.)," "To Antiohos Epifanis," and "Temethos, Antiochian, 400 C.E."

THOSE WHO FOUGHT FOR THE ACHAIAN LEAGUE

Written 1922, printed 1922.

In this historical poem, the imaginary protagonist writes in about 110 B.C.E., about the defeat of the Achaian League or Alliance by the Romans in 146 B.C.E., which was the last futile attempt of the Greeks to keep their independence from Rome. There is an irony here, since by the time that the Achaian League surrendered to Rome, the heart of Greek arts and civilization was already alive in Hellenistic Alexandria, under the Greek Ptolemies (who were descendents of the early Macedonian generals and the Cleopatras). As for the history of the Achaian League, it went back, in 446 B.C.E., to a vague alliance between Athens, Sparta, and Macedonia against pirates and other enemies. It fell apart at the end of the fourth century B.C.E. after it split and fought Philip II of Macedonia in 338 B.C.E. The Second Achaian League was revived in 280 B.C.E., again as a force against the Macedonians. It fell apart when it included the Macedonians once more among them and the enemy was Sparta. Then in 198 B.C.E., the League joined with Romans against Sparta, which put most of the Peloponnese under their control. The ultimate tragedy, from the Greek point of view, came in 146 B.C.E. when the Romans defeated the Achaians at Corinth. With that victory Rome thereafter controlled Greece. Later wars were fought among Romans, to determine who would dictate law and authority in Greek lands. It is this last failure of the Achaians to which Cavafy refers in his poem for those who fought for the Achaian League.

To Antiohos Epifanis

Written 1911, with the title "Antiohos Epifanis," rewritten 1922, printed 1922.

Antiohos IV Epifanis (Antiochus IV Epiphanes) was the Seleucid (Selefkid) king of Persia from 175–165 B.C.E. The king's father was Antiochus III the Great. This poem, like so many by Cavafy, deals with the intrigues and shifting loyalties in the conflicts between the Seleucid Empire and the Macedonian and Ptolemaic alliances or enemies, depending on circumstance and year. Here the circumstance is Perseus, king of Macedonia, whose wife Laodice was the daughter of Antiohos's brother Seleucus IV Philopator (Selefkos IV Filopatros), who was murdered in 175 B.C.E. King Perseus tried once more to defeat the Romans and achieve independence, but he was defeated in 168 B.C.E. at the Battle of Pydna, which Cavafy refers to in the last line.

Antiohos Epifanis is probably best known for his infamous persecution of the Jews. See "Aristovoulos."

Tyre is Tyros, a commercial coastal city in Phoenicia, known for its purple dyes (Phoenicia means "purple"). Phoenicia is now a peninsula of Beirut in Lebanon.

For more on Antiohos, see "The Battle of Magnesia," "Of Dimitrios Sotir (162–150 B.C.E.)," and "Temethos, Antiochian, 400 C.E."

In an Old Book—

Written 1892, with title "The Book," printed 1922.

In Despair

Written 1923, printed 1923.

Edmund Keeley and Philip Sherrard, translators of George Seferis's (1900–1971) collected poems, note that the Greek Nobel laureate remarked that the musical effect of this poem is that of a popular tango (C. P. *Cavafy*, p. 251).

From the Drawer

Written 1923, unpublished.

Julian Seeing Indifference

Written 1923, printed 1923.

The beginning quotation in the poem is from a letter written in 363 C.E. in which Theodorus is appointed High Priest of Asia.

Galatia, as in Paul's Letter to the Galatians, refers not to the Galatia in Western Europe but to the provinces of Phrygia and Cappadocia, now in central Turkey and west toward the Mediterranean coast.

In all these poems concerning Julian, there is an ironic tone in which the imaginary protagonist speaks with some scorn for Julian's paganizing efforts. Cavafy leaves us uninformed what his own position is, which has led some commentators to state that Cavafy is writing these poems in order to reject Julian. Cavafy's preoccupation with Julian, devoting so much attention to him, in itself weakens the argument of rejection. Also, Cavafy's almost salvific turn to paganism in such poems as "Of the Jews" and "Myris: Alexandria, 340 C.E." places Cavafy among admirers of pagan classical philosophy and culture.

For more on Julian, see "Julian at the Mysteries," "Julian in Nikomedia," "A Grand Procession of Priests and Laymen," "You Did Not Know," and "In the Suburbs of Antioch."

Epitaph of Antiohos, King of Kommagini

Written 1923, printed 1923.

The characters and epitaph are invented by Cavafy. The reference is probably to Antiohos I, King of Kommagini (Antiochus I, King of Commagene) (ca. 69–30 B.C.E), who was called the Just, and who was friendly to Rome and the Greeks.

For more on Kommagini (Commagene), see "The Melancholy of Iason Kleandros, Poet in Kommagini, 595 C.E."

Theater of Sidon (400 C.E.)

Written 1923, printed 1923.

For more on Sidon and the date, see "Young Men from Sidon (400 C.E.)." The "jabbering of mortals" refers to the Christians.

JULIAN IN NIKOMEDIA

Written 1924, printed 1924.

The scene takes place in Nikomedia (Nicomedia), the port city and capital of Bithynia, a state in northwest Asia Minor, in present-day northwest Turkey. By 354 C.E., the time of this event, an original settlement of Thracians, later conquered by the Persians, was under Roman dominion of the Byzantine Empire. An example of Cavafy's irony is the opening couplet: "Wrong and perilous matters: / the praises for Greek ideals." Here, the imaginary protagonist is speaking in the voice of a Christian critic, whose words may be both for the fated Gallos (Gallus), Julian's half brother, who had been named to be emperor in 350, as well as Julian himself. The Emperor Konstantios II (Constantius II) was a devout Christian—and an Arian, which would later be decreed a principal heresy—and was suspicious of Gallos's nominal Christianity. In that year he had his nephew, Gallos, executed for his lack of religious beliefs. Julian was appointed as the imperial successor, though he did not actually ascend to the throne until 361.

Hrisanthios (Chrisanthios), meaning "gold flower," was a Neoplatonic philosopher and friend of Maximus of Ephesus (Efesos), a philosopher-teacher of Julian, who initiated him into magic rites. Mardonis, a eunuch, was Julian's Greek culture teacher.

For more on Julian, see "Julian at the Mysteries," "Julian Seeing Indifference," "A Grand Procession of Priests and Laymen," "You Did Not Know," and "In the Suburbs of Antioch."

BEFORE TIME CHANGED THEM—

Written 1924, printed 1924.

HE CAME TO READ

Written 1924, printed 1924.

IN ALEXANDRIA, 31 B.C.E.

Written 1917, rewritten 1924, printed 1924.

On September 31, 31 B.C.E., the fleets of Antony and Cleopatra were defeated in a major sea battle at Actium by Octavian, under the command of Agrippa. This event opened the way for Octavian's successful assault on Alexandria. Apparently, though here history may be gossip, Cleopatra attempted to save her fleet by fleeing, which guaranteed defeat. In any event, Cleopatra was not there to make such decisions. However, Cleopatra arranged a triumphant return to Alexandria, to hide the defeat from her subjects.

For more on Antony see "Antony's Ending," "The God Abandons Antony"; for Cleopatra see "Alexandrian Kings"; and for the sea battle see "In a Township in Asia Minor."

IOANNIS KANTAKOUZINOS TRIUMPHS

Printed 1924.

The fictional narrator worries about his plight because he has not backed the winning faction in a struggle for power. When the Byzantine emperor Andronikos III Palaiologos (Andronicus III Palaeologos) died in 1347, Ioannis VI Kantakouzinos (John VI Cantacuzenus) (ca. 1292–1382) was appointed regent and ruled jointly with the new lineal emperor, Ioannis V Palaiologos (John V Palaeologos), who was then only nine years old. Andronikos's widow, Anna, who was Anna of Savoy, a Frank, opposed Kantakouzinos's regency, and there ensued a civil war from 341 to 1347 between the two factions. Although French, Anna had the support of the Patriarch of Constantinople. Kantakouzinos won the struggle and was crowned Ioannis VI, and ruled jointly with his wife, Irini, Andronikos's sister. In 1354, John V Palaeologos forced his father-in-law to resign. Kantakouzinos then entered a monastery as a monk, and wrote his memoirs.

For more on Irini Assan, the granddaughter of the czar of Bulgaria, John III, see "Of Colored Glass."

TEMETHOS, ANTIOCHIAN, 400 C.E.

Printed 1925.

Temethos and Emonidis are imaginary characters of this love poem. The year 175 B.C.E. is the 137th year of the Royal Succession of the Greeks, originating from the Seleucid (Selefkid) Persian dynasty by Seleucus I (Selefkos I) (312–281 B.C.E.), who was one of Alexander the Great's generals. Samosata was the capital of Kommagini.

For more on Kommagini, see "The Melancholy of Iason Kleandros, Poet in Kommagini, 595 C.E." and "Epitaph for Antiohos, King of Kommagini." For the year 400, see "Young Men from Sidon" and "Theater of Sidon." On Antiohos Epifanis, see "To Antiohos Epifanis."

OF COLORED GLASS

Printed 1925.

The coronation of Ioannis Kantakouzinos (John Cantacuzenus) and Irini Asan took place in the church of the Vlachernai palace. The emperor and empress wore artificial gems, of colored glass, because the real crown jewels of the Byzantine Empire were pawned in Venice by Anna of Savoy to raise money for her struggle against Kantakouzinos. They were never recovered. See "Ioannis Kantakouzinos Triumphs."

THE TWENTY-FIFTH YEAR OF HIS LIFE

Written 1918, with the title "The Twenty-third Year of My Life, in the Winter," printed 1925.

ON AN ITALIAN SHORE

Printed 1925.

The figures and scene are imaginary. In the year 146 B.C.E. the Roman consul Lucius Mummius defeated the Achaian League at Corinth, which ended the hope of Greek independence from Rome. As the victor, Mummius behaved brutally, sacking Corinth, killing the men, auctioning the women and children as slaves, and razing the houses. The "spoils of Corinth" refers to all the art treasures of the city, which he stole and shipped to Italy.

IN THE BORING VILLAGE

Written 1925, printed 1925.

The poem takes place in a village in Egypt. The city is Cairo or Alexandria.

APOLLONIOS OF TYANA IN RHODES

Written 1925, printed 1925.

For Apollonios and Tyana, see "If Truly Dead." The long quotation is from Philostratos's *Life of Apollonios*, V, 22.

The Illness of Kleitos

Printed 1926.

In a Township in Asia Minor

Printed 1926.

The battle of Actium took place in 31 B.C.E. when Octavian's fleet defeated Antony and Cleopatra.

For more on Actium, see "The God Abandons Antony" and "In Alexandria, 31 B.C.E."

The Priest of Serapeion

Printed 1926.

Serapeion was the Temple of Serapis in Alexandria, built by Ptolemy I Savior (Ptolemaios I Sotir), 300 B.C.E. Then it was rebuilt by Ptolemy III Euergetes (Ptolemaios III Evergetis), 246–221 B.C.E. The Byzantine emperor Theodosius destroyed the temple in 391 C.E.

Serapis was an Egyptian god, who united qualities of the Apis bull and Osiris with parts of Zeus, Dionysos, Hades, and Asklepios. Some Gnostic sects saw him as the universal godhead. In Hellenistic times, and later during the Roman Empire, his worship was equal to that of other major Asia Minor and Mediterranean cults. The Ptolemies extolled him as the patron of Alexandria. Most of his priests were Greeks. The destruction of the temple by Theodosius was, like the Christian clergy's destruction of the great library, a catastrophe for classical letters, worship, and civilization.

See "Myris: Alexandria, 340 C.E."

In the Bars

Printed 1926.

A GRAND PROCESSION OF PRIESTS AND LAYMEN

Written 1892, with the title "The Cross," rewritten ca. 1917, printed 1926.

The procession is in Antioch, one of the early Christian cities, visited by Paul and Peter. It was founded in 300 B.C.E. by Seleucus I (Selefkos I), king of ancient Syria. The city, named for Seleucus's father Antiochus (Antiohos), a Macedonian general, soon became a rich commercial center by virtue of its location at the center of north, south, east, and west trade routes. It was occupied by Pompey in 74 B.C.E.

Antioch was a city of churches and magnificent ancient structures. It was also a center of Christian learning and played a significant role in the theological controversies of the time, especially with respect to the struggle between Paul and Peter as revealed in Paul's letters. Paul wished to open Judaism to the gentiles (the Greeks) by not requiring circumcision, and strict observance of the Sabbath and the dietary laws. Peter and the other apostles, John and James, in Jerusalem, fiercely opposed reinterpreting Jewish law or straying from its observance as prescribed in the Hebrew Bible. Ultimately, Paul prevailed, the Christian Jews multiplied, and eventually lost their first-century identity as a Jewish sect. Christianity (the Greek translation of Hebrew "messianism") flourished in Antioch, where it found its champion in Paul, who in his mission and letters almost single-handedly invented its later formation.

In Antioch, the Emperor Julian assembled his troops to fight the Persians. During a small battle, he was killed and the soldiers proclaimed his military commander, Jovian, the new emperor. Before his death, during his short reign of eight months, Jovian gave Christianity back the privileged position that it had held before Julian's turn to paganism and classical culture.

The Antioch area has been the site of many archaeological finds, including the "great chalice of Antioch," which some believed to be the Holy Grail, and at Daphne, Antioch's ancient suburban resort, beautiful mosaics from the first through sixth centuries, most copies of lost paintings.

See "In the Suburbs of Antioch."

A SOPHIST LEAVING SYRIA

Printed 1926.

An imaginary scene. For more on Antioch, see "A Grand Procession of Priests and Laymen" and "In the Suburbs of Antioch."

Julian and the Antiochians

Published 1926.

The epigraph is from the emperor Julian's satirical work *Mesopogon*, which means "Beard-Hater." The title is a bit of self-parody, since much fun was made of the emperor's beard. At the time, Antioch was a Christian city in which the moneyed classes exploited the peasants and slaves, and even contributed to their starvation during a drought, by charging them outrageously high prices for the grains they had themselves grown. In order to avoid famine, Julian imposed price controls. At the same time, he was also trying to institute a return to paganism. The upper classes revolted by resisting Julian's religious reforms. Instead of suppressing their dissent, Julian wrote *Mesopogon*, in which he disparaged the aristocracy for being egregiously pitiless and greedy while engaging in frivolous and hedonistic entertainment.

Regarding Julian's "childish fear of the theater," the emperor considered the theater shameful, and admonished pagan priests not to attend, nor to have any actor or dancer to their houses. Savidis notes that Julian stated he grew his "ridiculous beard" in order to "punish his face, which nature had made ugly."

For more on Julian, see "Julian at the Mysteries," "Julian in Nikomedia," "Julian Seeing Indifference," "A Grand Procession of Priests and Laymen," "You Did Not Know," and "In the Suburbs of Antioch."

Anna Dalassini

Printed 1927.

Alexios Komninos (Alexius Comnenus) came from a family of Byzantine emperors, who ruled during the eleventh and twelfth centuries; he reigned from 1081 to 1118. When Alexios went to war in 1081, he turned over the affairs of state to his mother, Anna Dalassini. Alexios's daughter, historian Anna Komnini, quotes the "golden bull" or imperial decree, in which her father officially makes her grandmother Regent of the Empire (*Alexiad*, III, 6).

Days of 1896

Written 1925. Printed 1927.

Two Young Men, Twenty-three to Twenty-four Years Old

Printed 1927.

Greek since Ancient Times

Printed 1927.

In Greek mythology, Io is the daugher of the river deity Inahos (Inachus), king of Argos. Zeus loved her and changed her into a white heifer in order to protect her from Hera's jealousy. Hera harassed her and chased her all the way to Egypt, where she died. Her brothers built a temple and a town, Iopolis, to honor her. That town became the capital of Syria and was renamed Antioch by Seleucus I Nicator (Selefkos I Nikator) in 300 B.C.E.

See Ovid's *Metamorphoses,* I, verse 748.

Days of 1901

Printed 1927.

You Did Not Know

Printed 1928.

For more on Julian, see "Julian at the Mysteries," "Julian Seeing Indifference," "Julian in Nikomedia," "A Grand Procession of Priests and Laymen," and "In the Suburbs of Antioch."

A Young Man, an Artist of the Word, in His Twenty-fifth Year

Printed 1928.

In Sparta

Printed 1928.

The outstanding king of Sparta, Kleomenis III (Cleomenes III), who reigned from 235 to 222 B.C.E., asked for help from his patron Ptolemy III (Ptolemaios III), in a war against the Macedonians and the Achaian League.

Ptolemy agreed, but demanded that Kleomenis's own mother, Kratisiklia, and his children be sent to Alexandria as hostages. Kleomenis initially succeeded, but then later was defeated. In 222 he fled to Ptolemy. He was imprisoned by Ptolemy's successor, escaped, and, failing to stir up a revolt in Alexandria, committed suicide.

The poem turns on the character of the hostage mother and her Spartan family, which traces itself back to Herakles, and considers the Lagidis dynasty of Ptolemies lowborn upstarts of Macedonian descent.

For more about the Ptolemies, see "The Glory of the Ptolemies."

PORTRAIT OF A TWENTY-THREE-YEAR-OLD MAN, PAINTED BY HIS FRIEND THE SAME AGE, AN AMATEUR

Printed 1928.

IN A LARGE GREEK COLONY, 200 B.C.E.

Printed 1928.

The colony and scene are imaginary. The date 200 B.C.E. is ominously close to two fatal dates, the battle of Cynoscephalae, when Philip V of Macedonia was defeated by the Romans in 197, and then, ten years away, the equally disastrous battle of Magnesia in 190.

See "The Battle of Magnesia."

A PRINCE FROM WESTERN LIBYA

Printed 1928.

The scene is imaginary. Libya was a general name for Africa.

KIMON, SON OF LEARHOS, TWENTY-TWO, STUDENT OF GREEK LETTERS (IN KYRINI)

Written probably 1913, with the title "Tomb of Marikos," printed 1928.

Kyrini (Cyrene) was the major Greek colony in Africa, a center of philosophers and poets, including the fifth-century B.C.E. philosopher Aristippus and the poet Callimachus (ca. 305–240 B.C.E), who was first cataloger of the library in Alexandria, an anthologist, and champion of the brief lyric epigram.

On the March to Sinopi

Written 1928.

Mithridatis V Evergetes (Mithridates V Euergetis), king of Pontos from 152 to 120 B.C.E., was the father of Mithridatis VI Evpator (Mithridates VI Eupator). The incident with the seer is imagined, but it refers to the actual event in which the elder Mithridatis is saved by his friend Dimitrios I of Macedonia.

For more on Dimitrios, see "King Dimitrios." For more on Mithridatis VI Evpator, see "Dareios."

Days of 1909, '10, and '11

Printed 1928.

Myris: Alexandria, 340 C.E.

Printed 1929.

340 C.E. was a time of political and religious turbulence in Alexandria. In 340, Constantine II (Konstantinos II) died in an ambush, when he invaded Italy in an effort to capture the territory of his brother, Constans I (Konstans). Alexandria was a center of the Arian controversy. Constantius I (Konstantios), their older brother who ruled Alexandria, was an Arianist. Constantine II held to his father's decree at Nicaea that Arianism was a heresy, and he was Orthodox (or Trinitarian). In 338, the Orthodox bishop of Alexandria, Athanathius, who in the course of his life was exiled five times, was granted permission by Constantine II to return to Alexandria, against the wishes of Constantius. Constantine's death in 340 meant that Athanathius lost his imperial supporter. In the same year, Athanathius assembled a council and condemned the Arians.

For a discussion of the dispute between Orthodoxy and Arianism, as well as a history of how the empire was divided between the sons of Constantine the Great after his death, see "Julian at the Mysteries."

For more on Serapeion, see "The Priest of Serapeion."

Alexandros Iannaios and Alexandra

Printed 1929.

Alexandros Iannaios (Alexander Jannaios) was king of Judea from 103 to

76 B.C.E., from the Hasmonean family of the Maccabees, who had liberated Israel from Syria by defeating the Selefkid Antiohos IV Antipatros (the Seleucid Antiochus IV Antipater). His wife Alexandra-Salome was the widow of his brother Aristovoulos I and the mother of Aristovoulos III, who was murdered as a teenager.

Judas Maccabeus was a Jewish priest and general, of the Hasmonean family, who, with his brothers Jonathan, John, Simon, and Eleazar defeated the Seleucids.

For more on the Hasmoneans, see "Aristovoulos," and on Greco-Jews, see "The Tomb of Evrion" and "Of the Jews (50 C.E.)."

BEAUTIFUL WHITE FLOWERS BECAME HIM

Printed 1929.

COME, O KING OF THE LACEDAIMONIANS

Printed 1929.

This poem continues the history told in "In Sparta." The quotation comes from Plutarch's *Life of Cleomenis*, XXVIII. After Kleomenis's (Cleomenis's) protector Ptolemy III (Ptolemaios III) died in about 221 B.C.E., and Ptolemy IV (Ptolemaios IV) succeeded to the throne, Kratisiklia was executed as well as Kleomenis's children.

See "In Sparta."

IN THE SAME SPACE

Printed 1929.

THE MIRROR IN THE FRONT HALL

Printed 1930.

HE ASKED ABOUT THE QUALITY—

Printed 1930.

THEY SHOULD HAVE CARED

Printed 1930.

The protagonist is an imaginary character, and the events take place between 128 and 123 B.C.E. The colorful names are nicknames for historical leaders.

Kakergetis means "malfactor," the ironic nickname of Ptolemy VIII Euergetes (Ptolemaios VIII Evergetis), whose name means "benefactor." He was also called Fiskon, meaning "bladder." Kakergetis was the father of Ptolemy IX (Ptolemaios IX), whose nickname was Lathyros, meaning "chickpea."

Zabinas, meaning "slave," was the nickname of Alexander II (Alexandros II), who was the supposed son of Alexandros Valas (Alexander Balas). Valas stole the throne of Syria from Dimitrios Sotir ("Savior"), holding the kingship from 128 to 123 B.C.E., when he was assassinated by Antiochus VIII (Antiohos VIII), who was known as Grypos, meaning "hooknose." Grypos reigned from 123 to 96 B.C.E., when he also was assassinated.

John (Yohanan) Hyrkanos, son of Simon (Shimon) Maccabeus, ruled Judaea from 134 to 104 B.C.E. The Maccabees were helped in their mission for independence by the chaos and murder that characterized the successions to the throne.

For more, see "Those Who Fought for the Achaian League," "Of Dimitrios Sotir (162–150 B.C.E.)," "The Favor of Alexandros Valas," and "Alexandros Iannaios and Alexandra."

According to the Recipes of the Ancient Greco-Syrian Magicians

Printed 1931.

In 200 B.C.E.

Written about 1916, with the title "Except the Lacedaimonians," printed 1931.

The date in the title places the poem close to the battle of Cynoscephalae (197 B.C.E.), when Philip V of Macedonia was defeated by the Romans and ten years from the battle of Magnesia. See "In a Large Greek Colony, 200 B.C.E."

The first line of the poem comes from an inscription Philip V had written on the three hundred suits of armor that he sent to the Parthenon in Athens.

Granikos (334 B.C.E.), Issus (333), and Arbela (331) refer to the three battles that decided Alexander the Great's (Megas Alexandros's) Persian campaign. While the Lacedaimonians (the Spartans) refused to participate in that campaign, it should be remembered that they had already been crushed militarily by their losses in 331 B.C.E. to the Thebans (Gaugamela) and in 338 B.C.E. to the Macedonians (Chaeronea).

Koine is demotic or common Greek, based on the Attic dialect, of the New Testament and popular literature. It was the lingua franca for at least six hundred years, in Mesopotamia (along with Aramaic), Asia Minor, North Africa, and Eastern Europe.

Bactria was a Persian satrapy (province) in what today is northern Afghanistan and southern Uzbekistan.

Days of 1908

Written probably 1921, with the title "The Summer of 1895," printed 1932.

In the Suburbs of Antioch

Written late 1932, early 1933. Published posthumously 1935.

Vavylas was bishop of Antioch from 237 to 250 C.E. He was a martyr and known as St. Babylas. He was buried near the temple and oracle of Apollo in a grove of Dafni (Daphne) at the order of Julian's half brother Gallus (Gallos). The priest of Apollo considered the temple desecrated by his burial and abandoned the temple, after which the Christians built a church over Vavylas's grave to honor their martyr. When Julian arrived in Antioch in 362, he ordered the church razed and Vavylas's bones exhumed for a purification ritual to take place. In 362, the shrine along with a famous statue of Apollo were destroyed by fire, which was blamed on vengeful Christians.

For more on Antioch, see "A Grand Procession of Priests and Laymen." For more on Julian, see "Julian, at the Mysteries," "Julian Seeing Indifference," "Julian in Nikomedia," "A Grand Procession of Priests and Laymen," "Julian and the Antiochians," and "You Did Not Know."

A NOTE ON THE TEXT, SELECTION, AND ORDER OF THE POEMS

This book contains Cavafy's complete published poems and a selection of the unpublished poems. The Greek text I used was *Απαντα Ποιεήτικα* (*Apanta Poietika—Complete Poems*) published by Ypsilon/Vivlia (Ypsilon/Books), Athens, 1999. The *Apanta Poietika* edition includes all the "Unpublished" and "Rejected Poems," many of which I chose not to translate because in my view they are not strong and are not the best representation of the brilliance of the poet. Readers who wish to read those poems can turn to the translations by Rae Dalven and Theoharis C. Theoharis, among others.

Traditionally, Cavafy's poems have been ordered chronologically and divided into the sections "Published Poems," "Unpublished Poems," and sometimes "Rejected Poems." I decided that it would give readers of Cavafy a better sense of the arc of his development to see all the poems together, chronologically, without regard to whether Cavafy had chosen to have them printed. The published poems are arranged according to the date of their publication or printing; the unpublished poems are interspersed with published poems, according to their dates of composition. For interested readers, here is a list of the unpublished poems included in this volume.

"Julian at the Mysteries"
'When the Watchman Saw The Light"
"The Enemies"
"Growing Strong"
"September, 1903"
"December, 1903"
"January, 1904"
"On the Stairs"
"At the Theater"
"Antony's Ending"
"Hidden Things"
"On Hearing of Love"
"'I Will Tell the Rest to Those Down in Hades'"

A BIOGRAPHICAL NOTE ON CAVAFY

Constantine P. Cavafy (Kavafis) (1863–1933) is one of the most important poets of the modern era. Born in Alexandria in 1863, he was from a prosperous family originally from Constantinople. From ages nine to sixteen, he lived in England where he learned English and acquired a love for English literature. The family moved back to Constantinople in 1882, in response to an anti-Christian and anti-European climate during which many were murdered. When a few months later things calmed down, the five older sons returned to Alexandria to resume their careers, while Constantine and his mother stayed in Constantinople. The family was separated for three years. Displacement and exile were experiences of his youth and became themes prominent in his work.

While living in his grandfather's home in Constantinople, Cavafy had immersed himself in Byzantine and ancient Greek history and continued his study of languages. In addition to English and Greek, he read ancient Greek, Latin, and Italian. (He read Dante in Italian.) He spoke French as natively as English, Greek, and Arabic. He became interested in demotic Greek (*demotiki*) and popular song at a time when official purist Greek (*katharevousa*) was stifling literature with its artificiality. The demotic language was a natural continuation of *Koine* (common biblical Greek) and Byzantine Greek. Although the vital spoken language of the Greeks was the demotic, newspapers, political speeches, business, and most literature was composed in *katharevousa*, and was beyond the reach of most people who were not privileged and highly educated. He began to write his first poems in Constantinople.

Then in 1885, Cavafy returned to Alexandria, where he would spend the rest of his life. In these years the family lost most of its wealth. Constantine spent his adulthood working as a clerk. He was later an assistant director of the irrigation section of the Ministry of Public Works, until he retired. He also earned occasional money as a broker on the Alexandrian Stock Exchange. These experiences of disenfranchisement, as a result of his family's fall from affluence and aristocracy, coupled with his homosexuality and his foreignness in each of his homes, whether in London, Constantinople, or Alexandria, give Cavafy a compassion and empathy for the outsider.

Cavafy was to be the great poet of modern Alexandria and of Greece, a nation rich in major modern poets, two of whom, George Seferis and Odysseus Elytis, would be Nobel laureates. The poet lived in a small apartment above a brothel on 10 rue Lepsius. There he lived, wrote, and received friends. Nearby was a Greek Orthodox church and a hospital. Michael Hagg wrote the following on the close friendship between E. M. Forster and Cavafy:

> Opposite was a hospital. Around the corner was a Greek Orthodox church. "Where could I live better," Cavafy said. "Below, the brothel caters to the flesh. There is the church which forgives sin. And here is the hospital where we die." It is possible that Forster may have first met Cavafy in the street, perhaps on the rue Missala that led to Cavafy's favorite billiard parlor, an encounter that Forster described in yet another book on the city, *A Novelist's Sketchbook of Alexandria through the Ages*: "The delightful experience of some who hearing their own name proclaimed in firm yet meditative accents that seem not so much to expect an answer as to pay homage to the fact of individuality. They turn and see a Greek gentleman with a straw hat, standing motionless at a slight angle to the universe."*

Cavafy is one of the world's preeminent poets, yet he never published a full-length book of poems publicly; he put out only selections of his poems every few years, privately, for friends, and published in a few journals. He had no difficulty circulating his poems in cosmopolitan Alexandria, a city, like Thessaloniki and Constantinople, of Greeks and diverse peoples. But in nationalistic Athens his troubled reputation even caused a lecture on his work to be called off. He would be known abroad, and with intense significance and influence, before being acclaimed in continental Greece.

In 1895 he met Periklis Anastasiadis; it was Anastasiadis who is responsible for promoting Cavafy in Greece, as well as introducing him to E. M. Forster. Like Emily Dickinson, Cavafy's larger audience came posthumously, but the smaller audience that he enjoyed while he lived was comprised of

---

*From a review article by the novelist/historian Amos Elon: " 'Alexandria: City of Memory' by Michael Hagg, Yale University Press," in *New York Review of Books*, May 26, 2005, p. 44.

powerful literary figures, especially in English. Forster carried his work to T. S. Eliot, Arnold Toynbee, D. H. Lawrence, and others. As a result, T. S. Eliot and Ezra Pound were profoundly influenced by his poetry, especially his ventures into history and myth. It is impossible to imagine Pound's *Cantos* without Cavafy (as Jane Pinchon and others have demonstrated). He continued to be a major influence in modern and contemporary literature. Greece's two Nobel laureates, George Seferis and Odysseus Elytis, were completely immersed in Cavafy, as was Yannis Ritsos. A short and most incomplete list of writers whose work reveals Cavafy's enduring influence would include W. H. Auden, Lawrence Durrell in his *Four Quartets*, Nobel Laureate J. M. Coetzee (whose well-known novel is entitled *Waiting for the Barbarians*), Marilyn Chin, Mark Doty (who gained fame with his book *My Alexandria*), Khaled Mattawa, and Carl Phillips.

In 1922 Cavafy retired from the Ministry of Public Works. He spent his days reading and writing, and entertaining friends in his small apartment. In the evenings he went to the neighborhood café where a circle of admirers placed him in their center. One such friend noted that Cavafy said, "Many poets are exclusively poets. . . . I, I am a poet historian. I, I could never write a novel or a play, but I feel in me a hundred and twenty-five voices that tell me that I could write history. But now there is no time." In June of 1932 he was diagnosed with cancer of the larynx. He would not accept the diagnosis until his condition worsened and, persuaded by friends, he consented to enter the Red Cross Hospital that July. He had a tracheotomy, which resulted in a temporary respite in the progress of the cancer—and in the complete loss of his voice. Early in 1933, he relapsed and entered the Greek hospital in Alexandria, where he would spend the last months of his life. He died on his birthday, April 29, 1933. He had no last words. In his last communication, he drew a circle, then put a period in the center.

INDEX OF TITLES AND FIRST LINES